Building Racial Competency in White Educators Through the Transformative Act of Writing

This book argues that the transformative act of writing can be used to strengthen the racial competency of White educators in profound ways, leading them to a more comprehensive consciousness regarding the way their racial identity impacts them personally and professionally.

Through detailing the experiences of two White educators who engaged in a practice of deeply reflective personal narrative writing about their racial identity, this book presents written data from the participants and discusses the theoretical and practical implications of the participants' written work. It also provides a strong, evidence-informed case for using reflective writing as a tool for strengthening the racial competency of White educators in order to positively impact their students, their classrooms, and their greater school communities. Lastly, the book offers writing exercises that can be applied to contexts within and outside the field of education so that readers can start the important work of further developing their racial competency.

It will appeal to researchers, teacher educators, faculty, and scholars with interest in whiteness studies and advancing antiracist pedagogies, as well as literacy education and diversity and equity in education.

Paul F. Walsh is a high school English instructor, professor of education at Lehigh University, and professor of education at Moravian University, USA.

Routledge Research in Race and Ethnicity in Education

This series aims to enhance our understanding of key challenges and facilitate ongoing academic debate relating to race and ethnicity in education. It provides a forum for established and emerging scholars to discuss the latest debates, issues, research and theory across the field of education research that pertain to race and ethnicity.

Books in the series include:

Family Engagement in Black Students' Academic Success
Achievement and Resistance in an American Suburban School
Vilma Seeberg

The Under-Representation of Black and Minority Ethnic Educators in Education
Chance, Coincidence or Design?
Christopher G Vieler-Porter

The Racialized Experiences of Asian American Teachers in the US
Applications of Asian Critical Race Theory to Resist Marginalization
Jung Kim and Betina Hsieh

British Indian Model Minority Pupils' Schooling Experiences
Attitudes, Attainment, and Strategies
Jatinder Kang

Building Racial Competency in White Educators Through the Transformative Act of Writing
Writing Through Whiteness
Paul F. Walsh

Building Racial Competency in White Educators Through the Transformative Act of Writing
Writing Through Whiteness

Paul F. Walsh

NEW YORK AND LONDON

First published 2024
by Routledge
605 Third Avenue, New York, NY 10158

and by Routledge
4 Park Square, Milton Park, Abingdon, Oxon, OX14 4RN

Routledge is an imprint of the Taylor & Francis Group, an informa business

© 2024 Paul F. Walsh

The right of Paul F. Walsh to be identified as author of this work has been asserted in accordance with sections 77 and 78 of the Copyright, Designs and Patents Act 1988.

All rights reserved. No part of this book may be reprinted or reproduced or utilised in any form or by any electronic, mechanical, or other means, now known or hereafter invented, including photocopying and recording, or in any information storage or retrieval system, without permission in writing from the publishers.

Trademark notice: Product or corporate names may be trademarks or registered trademarks, and are used only for identification and explanation without intent to infringe.

ISBN: 978-1-032-62397-9 (hbk)
ISBN: 978-1-032-65929-9 (pbk)
ISBN: 978-1-032-65930-5 (ebk)

DOI: 10.4324/9781032659305

Typeset in Times New Roman
by Apex CoVantage, LLC

Table of Contents

	Introduction	1
1	The Puzzle of Practice: The Necessity for White Educators to Reflect on Their Racial Lens	8
2	Theoretical Underpinnings: Whiteness, Antiracist Education, and the Transformative Power of Writing	16
3	The Study: Alex and Anna's Racially Reflective Journey	31
4	Whiteness as a Barrier to Developing Racial Competency in One's Personal Life	37
5	Whiteness as a Barrier to Creating Antiracist Educational Spaces	41
6	Combatting the Whiteness of Education Through Teacher Development and Through Classroom Instruction	46
7	Writing as a Way of Seeing and Being	50
8	Theoretical Implications and Implications for Teacher Development	56
9	A Lifetime of Critically Reflective Work: Swimming Upstream	70
	Index	75

Introduction

Unseen Implications of My Racial Identity: The Story of Jessica

I have always prided myself on the environment that I create in the classroom, one characterized by inclusion and valuing student voices from diverse backgrounds. I always saw myself as an educator who was not only interested in creating equitable classroom spaces but also as an educator who actually did the work in order to make these spaces a reality. Let me be clear: I did not come to the work in this book. It took me off guard and came to me. It came to me in the form of a student of mine who challenged me to reconsider the degree to which I was actually "doing the work" of equity, inclusion, and antiracist teaching. In many ways, I have her to thank for this book and for what I hope to be a lifetime of doing the work for real. And if there is one thing I have learned while on this journey, the only way to do the hard work as a White educator is to commit to it for a lifetime. This is something I will touch on in the conclusion of this book.

At the end of May 2020, I was preparing for a much-needed summer break. The COVID-19 pandemic had hit and thrust me into online teaching. I was away from my classroom. I was away from my students. I was away from my colleagues. I was away from the places and faces that make me excited to go to work every day with the hope of impacting people in a positive way. Coinciding with the disruption to education by the way of the pandemic was the murder of George Floyd. Because we were home all day every day, it was impossible to miss the gut-wrenching story from all angles. I taught a Politics of Writing course at the time, and I could not help but wonder how all of this was impacting my students. The video of the murder. The protests. The call for our government to act more aggressively to assure this never happens again. The general ignoring of this call. I remember watching the murder video for what seemed like the 1000th time, thinking, "I am not with my kids. I would usually shut everything down to help them process this. I want to send them all a message. But I don't want the message to come across as reductive or insincere. I will think about it." And think I did for a few days. But Jessica got to me first.

DOI: 10.4324/9781032659305-1

The following is the email I received from one of the students in my Politics of Writing course. Jessica is a Black young woman who took a very active role in our classroom conversations that focused on race, ethnicity, culture, gender, politics, and other social issues. She wrote with the subject line "Black Lives Matter":

Hi Mr. Walsh,

I cannot speak too soon because I am unable to know if you were already working on your response on behalf of George Floyd's death. As one of my teachers, I could always lean on you to hear my voice and validate it, that's how you are as a teacher and person. But I have to be honest with you Mr. Walsh, I was expecting you to share something with us. We share James Baldwin, Nikki Giovanni, Maya Angelou, and many others in your class. We are the history that will be taught in the future, and the importance is just the same. History this big cannot wait to be taught next year, we are in the midst of a revolution. I love your classes, and I admire the way you teach to make students know their voice is important. As for right now the voice of the allies and your voice is just as important. Your students need to hear from you Mr. Walsh. The power of one's voice is able to empower others to speak and a lot of staff members have been silent. As Elie Wiesel once said "We must always take sides. Neutrality helps the oppressor, never the victim. Silence encourages the tormentor, never the tormented"

I could lie here and tell you that my first reaction to this email was to put into motion immediate steps to repair my relationship with Jessica. But that was not my first reaction. My first reaction was one of anger. "I hope she sent an email like this to her other teachers who refuse to talk about any difficult topics in class," I thought. "She listed all the ways I have validated her in this email, so why would she come at me the *one* time I *may* have made a mistake. This is totally unfair of her." I was even ready to send an email back to Jessica capturing these sentiments in a more professional way. What would that have said about all the racial identity "work" I thought I had done? To this day I am grateful that I had better sense than to do this.

I ultimately decided to reach out to Jessica and suggested that we meet virtually to discuss her feelings. The conversation was respectful and eye-opening. I learned that Jessica saw me as one of the only White teachers who *seemed* willing to stand up in the face of racial injustice, and she was in disbelief that I remained silent. Jessica did not send me that email because she was angry with me; she sent me that email because she knew she could challenge me to do better as a White educator she trusted. This made me feel even worse. As a White teacher who *saw* himself as someone who indeed was able to be trusted by his students of color, it became clear to me that I could not be in one of the most pivotal moments of the young lives of my students of color. How serious was "the work" I thought I had done to reflect critically on my own racial identity if

I failed in this moment, a moment that so obviously called on me to do anything but stay quiet? How could I fail her this way? How could I fail all of my students this way?

The days and weeks went on. There was more and more about George Floyd on the news. Each night there was a new protest being covered on the news. Each time I came across anything related to George Floyd or the Black Lives Matter movement, I thought about Jessica. I thought about how she was looking to me, her White writing teacher, to provide support and allyship to her and her peers. What eventually struck me about this experience with Jessica is what inevitably brought me to this research. I had the privilege to wait to craft a response. I had the privilege to allow my thoughts and feelings to work themselves out. I had the privilege not to be a part of a community that was set ablaze by the murder of George Floyd. In short, I could take as much time as I wanted to—until Jessica called me out about what I claimed to preach in class but where I fell short when it mattered most.

Situating this Book in the Current Sociopolitical Context

It is imperative that I situate this book in the current sociopolitical context in order to best address the various issues that come with doing this work. The sociopolitical tensions that accompany doing race work in education are framed by the broader tensions of race in America. The fields of critical race theory (CRT) and critical whiteness studies (CWS) are under siege by the political right. The right deems the fields no more than liberal poison that create more racial division than racial unity. The right stands firmly by the idea of colorblindness, that the way to rid our country of racism is by not seeing color at all in an attempt to treat people equally. They say that theories like CRT and CWS do the exact opposite by defining people by their racial identities. In this way, advancing these fields of study is more important than ever. It is this colorblind ideology that allows White supremacy to go unnoticed and unnamed and remain an invisible structure that normalizes whiteness. To not see color is to willfully and purposefully deny the presence of whiteness and the inequitable systems that come with it. Being colorblind ensures that the White racial identity remains the unchallenged reference point for all that is "normal" and "good" about American education.

I also recognize that there are those who believe that any study of whiteness only further centralizes whiteness in ways that could potentially do more harm to communities of color and further entrench White dominance. However, I argue that in order to dismantle systems of White dominance, we must be able to name whiteness as a racial and sociopolitical identity. This should include putting it on display as something to be studied as a means to work toward a more equitable society without centering whiteness as the reference point for all things "normal." Ironically, we have to analyze the ways that whiteness has been the reference point for a "normal," "American" way of life in order to dismantle it as a reference point at all.

It goes without saying that there are a myriad of complex issues that come with White people doing any work at all in any field that focuses on race. Some people believe White people should not even be doing race work. There is no doubt that the work of White people should always be accompanied by and in partnership with scholars of color who have lived racial experiences that White scholars simply have not lived. But while it cannot be denied that progress that has been made with regard to race in America has often been the result of the fearless leadership of people of color, this progress was also made in partnership with many White people. To deny White people entry into the study of and conversations about race is dangerous in a few ways. First, it denies White people potential opportunities to see the historical and current implications of their racial identity and transform their perspectives in order to work toward a more equitable world. White people must see the often invisible ways they have been in power, have remained in power, and the inequities that stem from being in power in order to even begin addressing these inequities. Second, denying White people the ability to do race work would not allow for the kinds of cross-racial partnerships that are necessary to create actionable and sustainable change on the grounds of race.

But something else is happening too, specifically within some of the communities of White people who are working to become more critically aware of their racial identity, its impact on them, and its impact on the people around them. At times, there seems to be a silent contest occurring, a race to see who can be "the most antiracist" or the most racially aware. This often comes with vilifying other White people who "aren't doing enough" or who "aren't getting it right" when it comes to racial identity work. I don't know if I can think of a situation that imperils the future of racial identity work for White people more than this.

Thandeka (1999) discussed the phenomenon of White-on-White abuse within the confines of White communities. She spoke to how White children learned early and often the dangers of even attempting to be more accepting and inclusive of cultures other than their own. With being more tolerant came the threat of abandonment by their White communities. In this way, White children learn that stepping beyond the boundaries of their White communities comes with the possibility of losing the stability that comes with being a part of that community. The result of this is clear and intentional: the maintenance of White dominance by blocking the ability for White children to see worldviews beyond their own.

While the abuse among people in "White antiracist" communities comes from a different place, I am not sure that the result is any different than that suggested by Thandeka's work. White people calling out other White people for not being "antiracist enough" or "racially aware enough" ultimately deters White people from continuing the work that is necessary to build racial competency and create more inclusive spaces. I am not saying that White people should not challenge their White peers to dig deeper into their racial selves, but to attack their peers who have taken on the difficult journey of building racial competency, to make them feel irredeemable in the face of a mistake, will result in their peers abandoning the journey in full.

What Jessica Taught Me

First, Jessica taught me that I was far from having "completed" my journey of developing my racial competency. Actually, she taught me that there is really no such thing as completing this journey. I will speak more to this point in the conclusion of this book. Secondly, Jessica taught me that the goal of her reaching out to me was not to make me feel guilt or shame. Rather, her goal was to authentically push me to consider the impacts of my racial identity beyond what I might have considered before. This is certainly one of the goals of this book and any authentically antiracist work: to ask White educators to think critically about their racial identity and how it impacts their experiences and the experiences of their students in the classroom.

I find it interesting, however, just how many people take issue with this specific call to action on the grounds of race. Ask a teacher if being a mother, a father, a coach, a son, a brother, a sister, a writer, an athlete, being poor, where they grew up, where they went to school, and so on impacts how they teach, how they respond to their students, and how their students respond to them. They will almost undoubtedly say yes. Yet, when asked if their racial identity impacts their experiences in the classroom, they might be less likely to admit this if they see it at all. A goal of this book is to ask White teachers to consider their racial identity as a critical part of who they are in the classroom just as they would any other part of who they are in the classroom. No one makes a White teacher feel guilty for how being a father impacts their classroom, and no one should make a White teacher feel guilty for how being White impacts their classroom. However, being White is just as important of an identity marker as being a father, even if it has not been critically considered before. This book is about learning how to think critically about this identity marker for no other reason than to be the best teacher one can be for their students.

Jessica also taught me another important lesson: I should expect to make mistakes on my journey to developing my racial competency as a White person. It did not come naturally to me to consider how being White impacts my life and the world around me. Unlike many of my students of color, I was not raised in a family that talked about the implications of my racial identity. To be honest, I can say with almost 100% certainty that my parents did not even think they had a racial identity. In this way, I had to work hard to learn (I am still learning and will always be learning) what it means to be White in American culture. This has not come without doing harm to people I care about, even if unintentionally, as in the instance of my experience with Jessica. However, intention and impact are entirely different things. While I did not intend to hurt Jessica and my students of color by waiting out my response to the murder of George Floyd, the impact did not match my intent; my silence signaled to them that one of the only White educators they felt they could trust was unwilling to speak up when it seemed to matter the most.

Jessica's *response* to my mistake taught me something too. Even though she was only a young junior in high school, she provided a model for what it should look like when unintentional harm is done by a White person to a person of color. She did not let me off the hook by saying that because I did not intend to hurt her, the impact did not matter. But while the impact was still a negative one, Jessica did recognize fully that I was not someone who was trying to hurt her. She explained to me the impact of my unintentional mistake and called on me to do better next time as a White adult she very much respected. She did not vilify me for making a mistake. She did not take to social media and cancel Mr. Walsh. She still saw me as an ally, albeit an imperfect one. And to her, not only was that okay, but it is to be expected as a White person who is authentically attempting to develop their racial competency.

Many White people fear making a mistake when it comes to issues of race, so they remain silent as opposed to saying or doing something that could result in their vilification. This is not an excuse. This is legitimate fear, and we have instances of this cancel and call-out culture almost every day in America across all media platforms. I have many White colleagues who would rather stay quiet than make a mistake that could jeopardize their job. Allow me to use an analogy about my young son to elaborate on this dynamic. It would be unfair and harmful to the relationship I have with my 5-year-old son if the first time he threw a baseball in the house, I screamed at him, made him feel guilty, and automatically sent him to his room without a conversation about how throwing a baseball outside is different than throwing a baseball inside. He might never throw a baseball in the house again. However, he might never throw a baseball *anywhere* again because of how I treated him. This would be a real shame, considering this is a sport he truly loves and wants to grow in.

I cannot expect my son to know all the rules of playing ball in the house innately; he is not only in his infancy as a baseball player but as a human being. Whether I like to admit it or not, when I met Jessica, I too was in the infancy of my racial identity development. In many ways I still am. But rather than treat me like I should know every mistake I could possibly make and avert them, Jessica treated me with respect as someone she knew wanted to do good but needed to do better. Now, if I explained the rules to my son over time and he chose to ignore them, that is a different situation entirely. I would have to change my tactic with him. The same could be said for Jessica. If we had five different conversations about the same issue and it was clear I was ignoring her, then she could no longer say I didn't know better; unintentional harm would seem to have transformed into intentional harm. If more people handled cross-racial issues with the grace, compassion, and intellect that 17-year-old Jessica did with me, I like to think we would make much more serious headway toward the goal of racial justice in the classroom and beyond.

At the Heart of This Book: The Transformative Power of Writing

My experience with Jessica thrust me into my doctoral program and jump-started my journey to becoming a more authentically racially competent White educator. This book chronicles a study I undertook with two of my former colleagues, Alex and Anna. Alex and Anna are both White teachers who see themselves as already racially competent but also willing to be more so. While I was interested in their experiences of growing up within the confines of largely White communities and teaching as White people, I was more interested in studying the tool we utilized to better develop their racial competency as White educators: personal narrative writing. It was the regimented and intentional act of writing over the course of months that allowed Alex and Anna to more fully understand the nature of their upbringing and the lens through which they saw the world. More importantly, however, it was the act of writing that made more permanent what they learned about themselves and moved them to make more active changes in their lives to become more racially competent people. I include the different writing exercises Alex and Anna completed during the study in this book. I also include a sample action plan for district-wide implementation of critical self-reflection on racial identity as well as the implementation of White educator inquiry groups. I hope that reading about the experiences of Alex and engaging with the exercises yourself will provide you with new insights that will aid you in your continued journey to become a more racially competent educator and human being.

Reference List

Thandeka. (1999). Learning to be white: money, race, and god in america. Bloomsbury.

1 The Puzzle of Practice
The Necessity for White Educators to Reflect on Their Racial Lens

Researcher Positionality

I am a White, cisgender, heterosexual male. I am the oldest of two children and come from a modest but middle-class background that afforded me a life where I wanted for virtually nothing. I played for the sports teams I wanted to play for. I always had enough money to go to the movies with my friends and grab a bite to eat. I never once feared walking home from the bus stop as a child. If my mother was not able to meet me at the bus stop, there was at least one other parent at the stop, one whom I knew well and who was ready to keep an eye on me. I went to Catholic school from age 4 through high school. I attended a public state university. While I was left with some debt, it was not the crippling sort of debt incurred by so many others, as my parents paid for roughly half of my undergraduate degree.

I am a father and a husband. My family and I followed along a similar path to my upbringing in settling into a middle-class neighborhood and enjoying a middle-class lifestyle. We go out to dinner when we want (for the most part) without having to fear being unable to pay another bill. While money is certainly tight at times, we have enough to send both my son and daughter to full-time daycare. While not always to the tune of a one-week all-inclusive destination, we do typically find a way to take a trip over the summer just to get away. I am a teacher, I am a writer, and I am a baseball coach, three roles that I take very seriously and understand the gravity that comes with the opportunity to influence people in these three positions.

I offer you this brief background to highlight that for the most part, I have lived a very privileged life. No life comes without personal struggle, but one thing is incredibly clear to me as I reflect on my life: never once have I had to answer to the color of my skin. I have never once been forced to consider the color of my skin as a variable in doing or not doing anything, entering or not entering a space, or being offered or denied an opportunity. Thanks to Jessica, I came to realize that it was all these qualities of my whiteness that allowed for me to have a lack of urgency as it related to supporting my students, something that I deemed myself a professional at doing. I had not been forced to consider how the color of my skin contextualizes my worldview and experiences in any real way until I received that email from my student. I have now come to see this critical reflection on the part of White educators as integral to creating more antiracist classrooms, schools, and districts. I came to learn the importance of all this through the eyes of my student, who challenged me to push beyond the work I thought I was doing.

The Whiteness of Education

In the 2017–2018 school year, 79% of public-school teachers in the United States were White and non-Hispanic (National Center for Education Statistics). As a White teacher, I want to uncover the often invisible ways that the racial identity of White teachers impacts their teaching and relationships with their students. My former school was a great place to study this because the staff there was almost 100% White, and the student population was over 70% White. As an arts school that preaches being open, tolerant, accepting, and inclusive, I wanted to investigate the ways in which the vast blanket of whiteness that shrouds the school does not allow it to be the things our school claims to be. I am not asserting this is some sort of intentional trickery or purposely filled with malice. I am asserting, however, that the American education system is largely a White, middle-class enterprise. Seeing that my school is perhaps even whiter than the average school, the teachers undoubtedly engage in this systemic whiteness of schooling whether they realize it or not.

We must do away with surface-level conversations that begin and end with confessions of White privilege if we want to create actionable change. A confession of White privilege is not the end game; it is not the antiracist act in itself (Lensmire et al., 2013). We must engage in work that has the goal of "making whiteness visible to everyone . . . [historicizing] the term . . . [showing] how the trope emerges in the seventeenth century, how it changes over time and place, and how it gets embodied differently within different bodies within different contexts" (Kennedy et al., 2005, p. 366). Asserting and seeing one's privilege functions as an important entry point to living a more antiracist life. However, "unfortunately, such confessions contribute little to dismantling the system of oppression that is the condition of privilege" (Applebaum, 2016, p. 9). In other words, we must investigate and challenge the systems that allow for these privileges in the first place.

In the specific context of education, White teachers must dive deeply into the self not simply to find their privileges but, more importantly, to uncover the various parts of the complex system that gave them these privileges in the first place, a system they are a part of and must constantly be aware they are a part of. This second wave of CWS "understands that whiteness is a hegemonic racial structure, and white identity is intersectional 'and often privileged but does not totalize, reduce, or essentialize white identities to these important, however partial, understandings'" (Jupp et al., 2016, p. 5, as cited in Tanner, 2019, p. 186). White teachers must first become comfortable with seeing themselves as racial beings and discussing their whiteness as a racial structure. But this cannot be the end game; in the same way one cannot essentialize Blackness, one cannot essentialize whiteness. White teachers must move away from the external and refocus on the internal. This means teachers should not "always and only be looking to people of color in [their] learning or thinking about race" (Tanner, 2019, p. 184) and cannot "ignore or look past the *internal* conflict at the core of racial identity . . . 'the eternal battle by a self against itself in order to stop feeling what it is not supposed to feel: forbidden desires and prohibited feelings that render one different'" (Thandeka, 1999, as cited in Tanner, 2019, p. 183).

Significance of the Project: Writing as a Way of Being

In the words of Yagelski (2009), writing "can give rise to a conception of the self as autonomous and intellectual and thus may fundamentally change the relationship of humans to the world around them" (p. 10). He goes on to say:

> [T]herein lies the transformative power of writing, for when writing is practiced as an act of being, it opens up possibilities for individual and collective change . . . writing can become a vehicle to a deeper, more nuanced sense of ourselves as beings in the world.
>
> (p. 8)

Personal narrative writing is an excellent tool to use in order to move away from the external and engage in this deep dive of the self. This can lead to a personal transformation that can lead to transformation outside of the personal.

In short, I wanted to discover the ways in which being White and being a part of a White system of education impacts teachers personally and professionally and, thus, how it impacts their students and the greater school community. I wanted to identify specific ways that teachers can engage with their whiteness that might provide positive results in the classroom. One of the ways that I wanted to test how this can be done was through the writing of personal narratives and having open conversations with White teachers, where I asked them to think critically about their whiteness. Transformation starts at the personal level. I wanted to work with teachers to do just this so that it might become possible for them to transform their classrooms, their schools, and their greater communities.

My hope for my participants was that if their reflections and conversations were truly authentic, the teachers would take this newfound consciousness and put it into action by engaging in more sound and impactful antiracist pedagogies,

pedagogies that do not begin and end with a confession of privilege but rather "interrupt relations of racial inequality by enabling people to identify, name, and challenge the norms, patterns, traditions, structures, and institutions that keep racism and white supremacy in place" (DiAngelo, 2016, p. 330). I wanted to gauge the degree to which reflecting deeply and critically regarding the way being White has impacted them personally and professionally through the transformative act of writing would lead the teachers in my study to a more consistent consciousness of the way their whiteness impacts their students, their classroom, and their school.

Research Questions

In this way, the following research questions reflect the goals of my study, the problem of practice that grounds this study, and the theoretical underpinnings that guided the study:

1. How does writing personal narratives about race impact how White teachers process how their whiteness affects their personal experiences?
2. How does writing personal narratives about race impact how White teachers process how their whiteness affects their professional experiences in the classroom?
3. How does writing personal narratives about race affect the ability of White teachers to develop more holistic antiracist pedagogies?
4. How does participating in group meetings rooted in the discussion of their personal narratives about race impact the way White teachers process their whiteness personally and professionally?

Terminology

A common understanding of the following terms is critical to interpreting the various parts of this study:

1. **Critical Race Theory:** "the study and transformation of the relationship among race, racism, and power" (Delgado & Stefancic, 2017).
2. **Critical Whiteness Studies:** "Critical Whiteness Studies (CWS) is a growing field of scholarship whose aim is to reveal the invisible structures that produce and reproduce white supremacy and privilege. CWS presumes a certain conception of racism that is connected to white supremacy. In advancing the importance of vigilance among White people, CWS examines the meaning of white privilege and white privilege pedagogy, as well as how white privilege is connected to complicity in racism" (Applebaum, 2016).

3. **Whiteness:** "a term [that captures] all of the dynamics that go into being defined and/or perceived as white and that create and reinforce White people as inherently superior through society's norms, traditions, and institutions. Whiteness grants material and psychological advantages (white privilege) that are often invisible and taken for granted by Whites" (DiAngelo, 2016, p. 356).
4. **White Supremacy:** The "all-encompassing centrality and assumed superiority of people defined and perceived as White, and the practices based on this assumption" (DiAngelo, 2016, p. 356).
5. **White Privilege:** "A sociological concept referring to advantages enjoyed and taken for granted by Whites that cannot be enjoyed and taken for granted by people of color in the same context (government, community, workplace, schools, etc.)" (DiAngelo, 2016, p. 108).
6. **Antiracist:** "To be antiracist is to think nothing is behaviorally wrong or right—inferior or superior—with any of the racial groups. Whenever the antiracist sees individuals behaving positively or negatively, the antiracist sees exactly that: individuals behaving positively or negatively, not representatives of whole races. To be antiracist is to deracialize behavior, to remove the tattooed stereotype from every racialized body. Behavior is something humans do, not races do" (Kendi, 2019).
7. **Naming:** "coming to an understanding, through language, of the worlds we inhabit, how they work, how they relate to each other, how they account for diversity, and how they might do this better" (Harris, 2004).
8. **Racism:** "A form of oppression in which one racial group dominates others ... [this domination] is supported intentionally or unintentionally by institutional power and authority" (Diangelo, 2016, p. 108).
9. **Racial Competence:** "having the skills and confidence to engage in healthy and reciprocal cross-racial relationships; to recognize and honor difference without judgement; to notice and analyze racial dynamics as they occur; to confront racism at the individual, group, and systems level; to cultivate support mechanisms for continuing to be involved in antiracist practice even when it is discouraging or conflictual; to speak one's mind and be open to feedback on one's ideas; to ask for feedback about one's ideas and work; and to raise race questions about oneself and one's practice" (Michael, 2015, p. 5).
10. **Racial Self-Inquiry:** "a process of constant engagement with a question, a commitment to sit with a difficult query and to keep asking over time ... a rigorous and systematic process of research, experimentation, and community building around challenging dilemmas" (Michael, 2015, p. 2). In this case, the "difficult query" and "challenging dilemma" is that of one's racial identity.

11. **Positive White Racial Identity:** "does not mean feeling good about being White . . . it means having an understanding of what it means to be White in a society that historically, contemporarily, and systemically favored whiteness above other races" (Michael, 2015, p. 4).

Theoretical Framework

This research is grounded largely in the field of CWS, a field that aims to "reveal the invisible structures that produce and reproduce White supremacy and privilege" (Applebaum, 2016, p. 1). Scholars in the field "seek to make explicit the ways in which whiteness is a determinant of social power and to demonstrate how whiteness works through its invisibility" (Applebaum, 2016, p. 2). While this field makes up the majority of the framework that informed my study, the field of CRT is part of my larger theoretical framework as well. CRT scholars seek to "study and transform the relationship among race, racism, and power" (Delgado & Stefancic, 2017, p. 3). Seeing as CWS developed out of the field of CRT, it too is an integral part of my theoretical framework.

Methodologically speaking, my study is framed by the process of narrative inquiry. I asked my participants to engage in narrative self-inquiry, specifically a type of racial storytelling (Johnson, 2017) where they were asked to tell the story of how their race has impacted and continues to impact them personally and professionally. I recounted these racial stories and the stories of their experiences in the study by utilizing narrative inquiry. These methodologies framed my study because at the core of the study lie the acts of "living, telling, retelling, and reliving" (Clandinin, 2016, p. 34).

Lastly, in the act of writing personal narratives, my study is framed by the theory that writing has the potential to lead to personal transformation for the writer and, thus, a transformation of the world that surrounds the writer (Yagelski, 2009). Engaging with the genre of personal narrative can allow writers to come to a better understanding of the impact that transcendent experiences have had on their lives (Raab, 2014). In the context of my study, I believe that the penning of authentic and reflective personal narratives can result in White teachers coming to a fuller understanding of their racial selves and can strengthen their racial competency. This will improve not only their role as an educator but also the various roles they play in their lives outside of their classrooms.

This is but a brief description of the theoretical framework that guided my study. The subsequent literature review fleshes out the various parts of my theoretical framework in much greater detail, where I will position my study in the broader scope of the research of the authors cited above in conjunction with many others.

Situating the Study in the Current Sociopolitical Context

Lastly, I recognize the complex issues that come with White people doing any work at all in any field that focuses on race. There is no doubt that the work of White people should always be accompanied by and in partnership with scholars of color who have lived racial experiences that White scholars simply have not lived. But while it cannot be denied that any progress that has been made with regard to racial equity in America has often been the result of the fearless leadership of people of color, this progress was also made in partnership with many White people. To deny White people entry into the study of and conversations about race is dangerous in a few ways. First, it denies White people potential opportunities to see the historical and current implications of their racial identity and transform their perspectives in order to work toward a more equitable world. White people must see the often invisible ways they have been in power, have remained in power, and the inequities that stem from being in power in order to even begin addressing these inequities. Second, denying White people the ability to do race work would not allow for the kinds of cross-racial partnerships that are necessary to create actionable and sustainable change on the grounds of race.

Reference List

Applebaum, B. (2016, June 9). *Critical whiteness studies.* Oxford Research Encyclopedia of Education. https://oxfordre.com/education/view/10.1093/acrefore/9780190264093.001.0001/acrefore-9780190264093-e-5

Clandinin, J. D. (2016). *Engaging in narrative inquiry.* Routledge, Taylor & Francis Group.

Delgado, R., & Stefancic, J. (2017). *Critical race theory: An introduction* (3rd ed.). New York University Press.

DiAngelo, R. (2016). *What does it mean to be white? Developing white racial literacy.* Peter Lang.

Harris, R. (2004). Encouraging emergent moments: The personal, critical, and rhetorical in the writing classroom. *Pedagogy: Critical Approaches to Teaching Literature, Language Composition, and Culture, 4*(3), 401–418.

Johnson, L. L. (2017). The racial Hauntings of one black male professor and the disturbance of the self(ves): Self-Actualization and racial storytelling as pedagogical practices. *Journal of Literacy Research, 49*(4), 476–502. https://doi.org/10.1177/1086296x17733779

Jupp, J. C., Berry, R. T., & Lensmire, T. J. (2016). Second-wave white teacher identity studies: A review of white teacher identity literatures from 2004 through 2014. *Review of Educational Research, 86*(4), 1151–1191. https://doi.org/10.3102/0034654316629798

Kendi, I. X. (2019). *How to be an antiracist.* One World.

Kennedy, T. M., Middleton, J. I., & Ratcliffe, K. (2005). The matter of whiteness: Or, why whiteness studies is important to rhetoric and composition. Rhetoric Review, 24(4), 359–373.

Lensmire, T., Mcmanimon, S., Tierney, J. D., Lee-Nichols, M., Casey, Z., Lensmire, A., & Davis, B. (2013). McIntosh as synecdoche: How teacher education's focus on white privilege undermines antiracism. Harvard Educational Review, 83(3), 410–431.

Michael, A. (2015). *Raising race questions: Whiteness and inquiry in education*. Teachers College Press.

Raab, D. (2014). Creative transcendence: Memoir writing for transformation and empowerment. *The Journal of Transpersonal Psychology, 46*(2), 1–21.

Tanner, S. J. (2019). Whiteness is a white problem: Whiteness in English education. *English Education, 51*(2), 182–198.

Thandeka. (1999). *Learning to be white: Money, race, and god in America*. Bloomsbury.

Yagelski, R. P. (2009). A thousand writers writing: Seeking change through the radical practice of writing as a way of being. *English Education, 42*(1), 6–28.

2 Theoretical Underpinnings

Whiteness, Antiracist Education, and the Transformative Power of Writing

Review of the Literature

This literature review provides an in-depth discussion of the theories, concepts, and methodologies that guided the study while I position the study within the broader scope of the existing research. In terms of organizational structure, the first half of the literature review consists of a discussion of CRT and CWS, the two major frameworks that grounded my study on a theoretical level. I give an overview of the major aims of the theories. I then move on to a discussion of the major concepts/assumptions that undergird the theories. Lastly, I review research that applies the concepts/assumptions of the theories to the field of education specifically.

The second half of the literature review consists of a discussion of research regarding the methodological approaches I took in conducting this study. I discuss the process of self-inquiry, specifically the act of racial storytelling (Johnson, 2017). Seeing as this is a process, I asked my participants to engage with it in a rather in-depth way. I then discuss the methodology of narrative inquiry, which I utilized in recounting the personal and professional stories my participants shared regarding their race as well as the stories of my participants as they related to their experiences in being part of my study. I end the literature review by discussing research that suggests the act of writing has the potential to be transformative for the writer on a personal level and thus comes also with the potential for the writer to change the world around them.

Critical Race Theory

CRT originated in the 1970s when "a number of lawyers activists, and legal scholars across the country realized, more or less simultaneously, that the head advances of the civil rights era of the 1960s had stalled and, in many respects, were being rolled back" (Delgado & Stefancic, 2017, p. 4). Seminal works like "Serving Two Masters: Integration Ideals and Client Interests in School Desegregation Litigation" (Bell, 1995a [1976]), "Brown v. Board of Education and the

Interest-Convergence Dilemma" (Bell, 1995b [1980]), and "Legitimizing Racial Discrimination through Antidiscrimination Law: A Critical Review of Supreme Court Doctrine" (Freeman, 1995) set the stage for what would become a flourishing movement where scholars aimed to "study and transform the relationship among race, racism, and power" (Delgado & Stefancic, 2017, p. 3). Delgado and Stefancic (2017) summarize the major tenets that most CRT practitioners would agree on:

1. Racism is ordinary, not aberrational.
2. We live in a society that privileges White over Color. Thus, racism advances White elites (materially) and the White working class (psychically).
3. Race is a product of social thought and relation.
4. Different minority groups have been racialized at different times throughout history by dominant society to suit their purposes.
5. Every person has a multiplicity of identities (political, ethnic, cultural, gender, sexuality, socioeconomic class, etc.) that work together, compete, overlap, and so on. In this way, CRT is rooted in intersectionality.
6. Minority status brings with it a presumed competence to speak about race and racism.

The field of CRT came to take hold across a wide range of disciplines, including that of education. CRT as a pedagogical practice aims to help students "achieve a critical understanding of the role of race and racism in society" (Ledesma & Calderón, 2015, p. 210), in order to "empower students of color while dismantling notions of colorblindness, meritocracy, deficit thinking, linguicism, and other forms of subordination" (p. 208). CRT educational theorists see "the official school curriculum as a culturally specific artifact designed to maintain a White supremacist master script" (Ladson-Billings, 1998, p. 18). In this way, CRT educational theorists see education as yet another expansive system that maintains and perpetuates a White supremacist ideology through tools unique to its discipline, such as curriculum, student discipline, teacher instruction, achievement tests, and school funding, to name only a few.

Critical Whiteness Studies

CWS is a

> growing field of scholarship whose aim is to reveal the invisible structures that produce and reproduce White supremacy and privilege. Scholars in the field seek to make explicit the ways in which whiteness is a determinant of social power and to demonstrate how whiteness works through its invisibility.
> (Applebaum, 2016, pp. 1–2)

I briefly outlined the field of CRT and its major tenets because the field of CWS grew out of the field of CRT; the field of CWS utilizes the major assumptions of CRT as a basis for its own areas of exploration. While CWS is the primary theoretical framework that I utilized to guide my dissertation study, CRT provides the groundwork for the field of CWS—thus, it must be considered a part of my broader theoretical framework.

CWS took hold in the 1990s with the work of scholars like David Roediger (1991), Peggy McIntosh (1997 [1988]), and Ruth Frankenberg (1997) (as cited in Leonardo, 2009). This first wave of CWS focused heavily on the concept of White privilege. While a discussion of privilege must be a part of any discussion of whiteness, it does not define the White racial identity in full. In recent years, this second wave of CWS has shown that a confession of White privilege is not the end game; it is not the penultimate antiracist act in itself. Contemporary CWS scholars believe that there must be a shift away from this first wave of CWS that focused so much on confessions of White privilege. A second-wave CWS "does not totalize, reduce, or essentialize White identities to these important, however partial, understandings" (Jupp et al., 2016, p. 1154). While understanding one's privilege is important on some level and is perhaps an entry point, "unfortunately, such confessions contribute little to dismantling the system of oppression that is the condition of privilege" (Applebaum, 2016, p. 9). This second wave of CWS aims to focus more specifically on

> making whiteness visible to everyone . . . [historicizing] the term . . . [showing] how the trope emerges in the seventeenth century, how it changes over time and place, and how it gets embodied differently within different bodies within different contexts.
>
> (Kennedy et al., 2005, p. 366)

This more nuanced and complex approach to the study of whiteness leads to a more authentically antiracist society.

While the White-led CWS movement of the 1990s created a more formal collection of ideologies that came to form the movement, this was hardly the first time anyone theorized whiteness. Before moving into a more robust discussion of the concerns of CWS scholars, it is important to discuss the movement's roots in the scholarship of Black theorists and writers. Veronica T. Watson, in her book *The Souls of White Folk: African American Writers Theorize Whiteness* (2013), artfully chronicles the tradition "within African American literature in which authors explore Whiteness as a racialized subjectivity" (p. 5). In her book, Watson shows how the work of thinkers such as W.E.B. Dubois, Charles Chestnutt, James Baldwin, Zora Neale Hurston, Toni Morrison (to name merely a few) were some of the first to discuss whiteness and its implications in critical ways, thus laying the groundwork for what would become the CWS movement.

Baldwin discussed the necessity for the White man to be "released from the tyranny of his mirror" (*The Fire Next Time*, 1993, p. 95), which he seems unprepared to do because the White man does not

> believe my version of the story, believe that it happened ... [and] in order to avoid believing that, they have set up in themselves a fantastic system of evasions, denials, and justifications, which system is about to destroy their grasp of reality, which is another way of saying their moral sense.
> ("The White Problem," 1964, as cited in Watson, 2013, p. 15)

Dubois said, "We who are dark can see America in a way that White Americans cannot" ("Criteria of Negro Art," 1926, as cited in Watson, 2013, p. 3). In *Black Skin, White Masks*, Frantz Fanon said, "what is called the black soul is a construction of white folk" (2008, p. xviii). Toni Morrison asked the question, "What happens to the writerly imagination of a black author who is at some level *always* conscious of representing one's own race to, or in spite of, a race of readers that understands itself to be 'universal' or 'race-free'" (1992, p. xi.). The words of these Black writers and so many others have "helped us to understand Whiteness more deeply and fully than perhaps we thought possible" (Watson, 2013, p. 11). In this way, the field of CWS owes a great amount of debt to the great Black thinkers who have been theorizing whiteness for years and whose ideas concerning whiteness make up the foundation of CWS.

Whiteness and the White Racial Identity

While there are a myriad of definitions for whiteness, I will use the one offered by Robin DiAngelo (2016), as I find that it speaks to the multiplicity of layers that comprise the White racial identity. She says whiteness is

> a term [that captures] all of the dynamics that go into being defined and/ or perceived as White and that create and reinforce White people as inherently superior through society's norms, traditions, and institutions. Whiteness grants material and psychological advantages (White privilege) that are often invisible and taken for granted by Whites.
> (p. 356)

Worth noting in this definition is the word "perceived." In other words, someone who does not define themselves as White may indeed reap all the benefits of whiteness if society views them as White. These shifting views of what it means to be White make whiteness difficult to pin down and articulate in full.

There is no doubt that White people's inability to readily see the privileges afforded to them just by being White is incredibly problematic. But another aspect of Whiteness that poses problems between White people and people of color and leads to the invisibility of whiteness is the degree to which White people often ignore whiteness as a racial category in full, that somehow being White equates to being "raceless" and any other person of color is "filled with race." CWS scholars and practitioners aim to make visible the intricate ways that whiteness as a racial identity plays in shaping the lives of White people. This allows White people to see how they "fit into the larger conversation about race" (Michael, 2015, p. 3). Critical to the field of CWS is the understanding that White people do indeed have a racial identity and that having this racial identity affects the way White people interact with the world and, in turn, the way that the world interacts with them.

The Normalization of Whiteness, White Supremacy, and White Privilege

Ruth Frankenberg (1997), a pioneer of CWS, further articulates the ultimate dangers of White people, characterizing their whiteness as "raceless" and "cultureless." Denying the culture of whiteness and the White racial identity results in the perpetuation of White domination and the use of whiteness as the point of comparison for what is deemed "normal" in American society. Frankenberg suggests that we must engage in discussions about whiteness as a culture and racial identity with a deep-rooted history in order to "dislodge the claims to rightful dominance" (p. 633) that White people wittingly and unwittingly make. This dominance leads to the notion that whiteness should be the reference point to which everything else is compared. In this way, people of color are not only people of color; they are also "un-white." In their being defined by what they are not (White), they come to be characterized as the abnormal "Other."

When Frankenberg talks about dominance, she is speaking to the dominance that results from the deeply entrenched ideology of White supremacy that has come to characterize American society and positions whiteness as the "normal" standard against which everything else is compared. In her essay "Representing Whiteness in the Black Imagination" (1992), bell hooks discusses the term "White supremacy," a term that she sees as much more useful when describing the way that people of color experience the world. She says:

> In a white supremacist society, white people can 'safely' imagine that they are invisible to black people since the power they have historically asserted, and even now collectively assert over black people, accorded them the right to control the black gaze.
>
> (p. 340)

In hooks' view, White supremacy does not always take the face of Ku Klux Klan members marching, White nationalists gathering to threaten Black Lives

Matter supporters with guns, or White terrorists storming the Capitol. While these examples are certainly overt acts of White supremacy, the ways a country built on the premise of White supremacy expresses this ideology are not always so obvious.

Put the way hooks describes, White supremacy becomes a term that reflects the "all-encompassing centrality and assumed superiority of people defined and perceived as white, and the practices based on this assumption" (DiAngelo, 2016, p. 356). In citing Charles W. Mills' *The Racial Contract* (1997), Robin DiAngelo says that Mills describes White supremacy as "the unnamed political system that has made the modern world what it is today" (DiAngelo, p. 146). In allowing this ideology of White supremacy to go unnamed and unchecked for centuries, a pervasive system of "White domination" was created that is held up by an "assumed [White] superiority that legitimizes it" (DiAngelo, p. 147). These unchallenged assumptions of White superiority are built into the fabric of American society in many subtle ways, thus resulting in the general acceptance of whiteness as the "normal" standard for living. It is critical to understand the sweeping magnitude of the system of domination that has created White supremacy throughout the course of history in order to fully utilize the lens of CWS.

Peggy McIntosh's essay titled "White Privilege and Male Privilege: A Personal Account of Coming to See Correspondences through Work in Women's Studies" (1997 [1988]) is recognized as a seminal essay in the development of the concept of White privilege. In describing the concept of White privilege, McIntosh uses the metaphor of a knapsack. She says:

> I have come to see white privilege as an invisible package of unearned assets that I can count on cashing in each day, but about which I was "meant" to remain oblivious. White privilege is like an invisible weightless knapsack of special provisions, assurances, tools, maps, guides, codebooks, passports, visas, clothes, compass, emergency gear, and blank checks.
> (1997 [1988], p. 2)

On one hand, this definition is useful as it shows the invisible nature of the many privileges of White people. Thinking critically about these invisible privileges is necessary in order for a White person to start to see the degree to which their racial identity affects the way they experience the world. However, McIntosh's definition is potentially damaging in its use of the words like "unearned," "oblivious," and "weightless." These words come across as rather passive. In one way, I suppose this makes sense, seeing as she is describing the phenomena of an invisible set of privileges afforded to a certain group of people. However, in the passivity of these terms also lies something dangerous: the assumption that these privileges were not the result of anything being violently stripped from or done unto another group in order to attain them.

I chose to discuss the concepts of White supremacy and White domination before delving into the concept of White privilege for this exact reason; the concept of White privilege is inextricably tied to the concepts of White supremacy and White dominance. In his book *Race, Whiteness, and Education* (2009), Zeus Leonardo says, "the conditions of white supremacy make white privilege possible . . . in order for white racial hegemony to saturate everyday life, it has to be secured by a process of domination" (p. 75). Leonardo's concern is that discourses of White privilege often "obscure the subject of domination . . . because the situation is described almost as happening without the knowledge of whites" (p. 76). To return to McIntosh's metaphor of the knapsack, I would argue that just because privileges are "invisible" to someone does not mean that they were attained without any action or force. Leonardo echoes this point, saying, "Privilege is the daily cognate of structural domination. Without securing the latter, the former is not activated" (p. 88). While I have discussed the issue of discourses of White privilege potentially ignoring the White supremacy and White domination that result in the privilege on a general level in this section, I will discuss the impact this issue has in the field of education, namely in the field of antiracist education, in the subsequent section.

Antiracist Education and CWS

Ibram X. Kendi defines the term antiracist as

> [thinking] nothing is behaviorally wrong or right—inferior or superior—with any of the racial groups. Whenever the antiracist sees individuals behaving positively or negatively, the antiracist sees exactly that: individuals behaving positively or negatively, not representatives of whole races. To be antiracist is to deracialize behavior, to remove the tattooed stereotype from every racialized body. Behavior is something humans do, not races do.
>
> (Kendi, 2019)

Antiracist education is not just about creating a multicultural classroom (Michael, 2015). While this is an important part of antiracist education, it is not the entirety of antiracist education. To return to McIntosh's knapsack metaphor, nor should the ultimate result of antiracist education be a pedagogy of privilege. A pedagogy that does not go beyond White privilege and investigate the systems of domination that allow for the privilege in the first place risks focusing exclusively on the individual. This focus on the individual "obscures the relational dimensions of privilege" (Applebaum, 2016, p. 7). This means that in focusing on White privilege on the individual level, a pedagogy of White privilege does not name the intricate ways that Whites are "interdependent upon the constitution of racialization of others through unjust social and historical processes" (p. 7). In the same way that discourses of White privilege can result in a limited view of White racial identity on a general level (due to the potential of ignoring White supremacy and White domination as prerequisites for privilege), pedagogies that start and end with White privilege can also be incomplete, if not damaging. There is no doubt that White privilege must be discussed as part of an antiracist education. However, it should never be discussed without also discussing the complex ways that allow the privilege to be and the active ways in which the privilege is perpetuated.

Robin DiAngelo defines antiracist education as "an educational approach that goes beyond tolerating or celebrating racial diversity and addresses racism as a system of unequal power between whites and people of color" (2016, p. 330). She goes on to say that the goals of antiracist education should be to "identify, name, and challenge the norms, patterns, traditions, structures, and institutions that keep racism and white supremacy in place" (p. 330). It is clear in these statements that centralizing whiteness is one of the keys to engaging in holistic antiracist pedagogies. "Centralizing" here does not mean making whiteness the rightful center of the universe; it means being critical of whiteness as the central location for racism and domination of minority groups. In citing Gilborn (2005), Bonilla-Silva (2001), and Mills (1997), Leonardo says that White supremacy has only recently come to be seen as a "social system that upholds, reifies, and reinforces the superiority of whites" (2009, p. 127). It makes sense then, as with any social system, that White supremacy affects a wide range of arenas. Education is not exempt from the dangerous implications of White supremacy. In this way, it is clear to see the usefulness of CWS as part of an antiracist educational model. Engaging in conversations in school about the vast implications of whiteness not only allows students and teachers to have a fuller understanding of the nature of racism in general but also allows them to see the ways that whiteness dominates the American education system.

So what are the ultimate goals of studying whiteness as a means to foster an authentically antiracist educational setting? Giroux (1997) says:

> Analyzing whiteness opens a theoretical space for teachers and students to articulate how their own racial identities have been shaped within a broader racist culture and what responsibilities they might assume for living in a present in which Whites are accorded privileges and opportunities (though in complex and different ways) largely at the expense of other racial groups.
>
> (p. 314)

In their review of antiracist studies in education from 2000 to 2015, Lynch et al. (2017) found that there were consistent aims in these studies: "(1) identifying or making visible systemic oppression, (2) challenging denial of [White] complicity in such oppression; and (3) ultimately transforming structural inequalities" (p. 135). They also found that these studies of antiracist education went beyond simply creating multicultural awareness or diversifying curriculum, nor did they promote a color-blind ideology by means of assimilation. These studies were unique in that they sought a "dismantling of the systems, structures, and institutions that keep racism in place" (p. 140). The authors found that across 15 years of scholarship in the field of antiracist education, an examination of whiteness and its implications was at the core.

CWS and Teacher Identity

I worked with teachers in this study. Thus, I focused on scholarship that places White teachers' conceptions of their whiteness at the center for this portion of this literature review. Jupp et al. (2016) conducted an extensive study of what they called "second-wave" White teacher identity studies. They define the field of White teacher identity studies as "a multidimensional field studying the cultural production of race, whiteness, and White teacher identities that articulates complex historical and social forces along with related understandings of teaching and learning in context" (p. 1163). First-wave White teacher identity studies "produced representations of the race-evasive and privileged identities of White teachers," and they paid little attention to how "these representations would then help or hinder future work with White teachers" (p. 1176). However, in their analysis of 65 studies out of this second wave of White teacher identity studies from 2004 to 2014, the researchers found that there was a "new emphasis in relation to race-evasive identities, careful attention to the nuances and complexities of White race-visible identities, detailed accounts of the actual pedagogies and curricula that form the complex contexts of White teachers' identities" (p. 1176). An investigation of this complexity of White identity is critical for White teachers who wish to engage in authentically antiracist pedagogies.

If the whiteness of teaching goes unexamined, White teachers will continue to reinforce the dominating racial ideologies of whiteness (Picower, 2009). In turn, this creates a situation where faculty and students of color are continually called on to "shoulder the work of antiracism" (Tanner, 2019, p. 195). White teachers must dive deeply into the self not only to discover their privileges; enacting a pedagogy of privilege as the end of the antiracist act itself will ultimately undermine antiracism (Lensmire et al., 2013). But in this inquiry of the self, White teachers cannot "fall back on their capacity to act as individuals, [thus] enabling them to retreat from the tensions produced by whiteness" (Levine-Rasky, 2000, p. 284). White teachers must seek to uncover the various parts of the complex system that gives rise to the privileges they enjoy. And they must see how this societal system frames the education system as well, a system of which they are an intricate part. Using CWS as a roadmap toward an authentically antiracist education means asking White teachers to *constantly* name and reflect on the various ways their racial identity affects their personal experiences, their experiences in the classroom, and the experiences of their students.

An Approach to Racial Self-inquiry for White Teachers

What does this investigation of whiteness on the part of White teachers actually look like? Whether explicitly or implicitly stated, the literature I have reviewed heavily favors Johnson's (2017) model of racial storytelling. While Johnson used this method to highlight his experiences as a Black male, Tanner used the model to "follow the lead of scholars of Color to engage with racial storytelling to resist white supremacy, even as I'm wary of reaffirming whiteness" (2019, p. 185). Tanner is certainly aware of the implications of utilizing the racial storytelling method of a Black man to tell the story of himself, a White man. However, Tanner also recognizes that "White people are haunted by race, too, whether it is recognized or not . . . therefore, I aim to tell honest, racial stories to grapple with the specters of my own racial hauntings" (2019). In Johnson's words:

> It is imperative for teachers to know themselves and understand how their racial past, present, and future shape their beliefs, values, and the multiple decisions they will make as teachers . . . as the majority of incoming education students are still White, it is crucial to analyze the impacts of whiteness. No White educator can simply ignore their own positionality and how it relates to their experiences and their perspectives on institutions.
>
> (2017, pp. 494, 496)

This reflection of the racial self allows White teachers to see the ways they are personally impacted by their whiteness and how their whiteness affects all aspects of their classroom.

Ali Michael (2015) would call this investigation of the racial self and the act of racial storytelling parts of the process of self-inquiry, "a process of constant engagement with a question, a commitment to sit with a difficult query and to keep asking over time" (p. 2). She calls this a "rigorous and systematic process of research, experimentation, and community building around challenging dilemmas" (p. 2). Michael conducted a study of six White teachers who participated in a race inquiry group. One of the main goals of this group was to help White teachers develop a more positive racial identity for her White participants. Michael says that a positive racial identity does not mean "feeling good about being White . . . it means having an understanding about what it means to be White in a society that historically, contemporarily, and systemically favored Whiteness above other races" (p. 4.). She goes on to say that "teachers cannot support their students to have a positive racial identity unless they as teachers already have a positive racial identity themselves" (p. 44). While it is not a perfect model because it does not describe every kind of White person, Michael utilizes Helms' (1995) White racial identity model to inform her understanding of her own development of a positive racial identity as well as those of her participants. A second primary goal of her race inquiry group was to help her White participants develop a stronger racial competence. She defines racial competence as

> having the skills and confidence to engage in healthy and reciprocal cross-racial relationships; to recognize and honor difference without judgement; to notice and analyze racial dynamics as they occur; to confront racism at the individual, group, and systems level; to cultivate support mechanisms for continuing to be involved in antiracist practice even when it is discouraging or conflictual; to speak one's mind and be open to feedback on one's ideas; to ask for feedback about one's ideas and work; and to raise race questions about oneself and one's practice.
>
> (p. 5)

Developing a strong racial competence is intimately connected to the goal of developing a positive racial identity.

The Transformative Power of Writing: Personal Narrative as a Tool for White Racial Self-inquiry

This study was influenced heavily by the work of Ali Michael as I ran my own small race inquiry group with the goals of studying the impact that participating in the group had on the development of my participants' racial identity and racial competency. I also wanted to study how the development of their racial identity and racial competency impacts their experience in the classroom. Michael's data was largely made up of observations during meetings and interview responses. I too facilitated group conversations regarding whiteness and race, took field notes during these meetings, and interviewed participants after their engagement with the study. However, I was particularly interested in studying the impact that the act of writing personal narratives had on the development of my participants' racial identity and racial competency.

Harris (2004) says that

> the composing and recomposing of reality and the self through language that happens in personal essays, autobiographies, and memoirs—to name only a few genres—is critical work. A student's own essay is a site for critical pedagogy to be enacted and for critical consciousness and social critique to emerge.
>
> (p. 402)

While Harris' focus is on the way that a teacher's engagement with student personal writing can be a place for teachers to actively engage in critical pedagogy with students, I argue that the same can be said for teachers working with other teachers. In this way, I asked my participants to write personal narratives over the course of a few months that called for them to consider the ways their whiteness has affected them personally and professionally. I asked them to write about the ways they are continuing to attempt to engage in more authentic antiracist pedagogy in their classrooms and to reflect on the results from a personal and professional stance. Lastly, I asked them to write about the role that our race inquiry group and the act of writing personal narratives played in the development of their racial identity and racial competency. How could the teachers in my study "come to an understanding, through language, of the worlds [they] inhabit, how they work, how they relate to each other, how they account for diversity, and how they might do this better" (p. 407)? How would my engagement with teachers and their personal narratives be a site for active antiracist practices?

The act of writing has the potential to be transformative for the writer and, thus, potentially transformative for the world around the writer. Yagelski (2009) says that "writing enables a kind of conceptual and analytical thinking that can give rise to a conception of the self as autonomous and intellectual and thus may fundamentally change the relationship of humans to the world around them" (p. 10). In her study of five accomplished memoir writers, Diana Raab (2014) examined the way that writing memoir impacted the authors' ability to process their transcendent experiences, or "an experience that goes beyond the ordinary" (p. 2). She found that memoir writing "led to a deeper understanding of the meaning of the transcendent experience and the role it played in their lives . . . writing about their lived experiences was a way for the participants to bring meaning into their lives" (pp. 18–19). The participants in Raab's study were "both transformed and empowered by the experience and process of writing a full-length memoir" (p. 19). Furthermore, the memoirists "connected with deeper reflections or illuminations about the [transcendent] experience and its role in the larger context of their lives, individually and in the universal perspective" (p. 19). In other words, the participants in the study found the act of personal writing to be personally transformative and thus found themselves able to apply what they learned through this transformation to the world around them.

While I did not ask my participants to write full-blown memoirs, I still aimed to examine the impact that the act of writing a personal narrative had on teachers as they explored their whiteness. Would the teachers in my study come to see their personal narratives as a way to "reaffirm and proclaim [their] being in the here and now" (Yagelski, 2009, p. 17)? Would the penning of the personal narrative result in personal transformation? If so, would this personal transformation result in the teacher's ability to transform their classrooms and the greater school community? These are the questions I sought to address regarding the role that authoring personal narratives might play in helping White teachers develop a more positive racial identity and a stronger racial competence.

Narrative Inquiry as an Approach for the Researcher of White Teacher Racial Identity

The teachers in my study engaged in deep self-inquiry comprising personal narratives, group conversations, and one-on-one interviews with me. However, as the researcher, I too had to find the appropriate avenue for telling the story of my participants' experiences in being a part of the study as a means to relay tangible results. In this way, I utilized a narrative inquiry approach to study the experiences of my participants. Jean Clandinin (2016) defines narrative inquiry as "an approach to the study of human lives conceived as a way of honoring lived experience as a source of important knowledge and understanding" (p. 17). In citing her previous work with Connelly (2000), Clandinin further describes the process of narrative inquiry, saying that

> it is a collaboration between researcher and participants, over time, in a place or series of places, and in social interaction with milieus . . . an inquirer enters this matrix in the midst and processes in the same spirit, concluding the inquiry still in the midst of living and retelling, the stories of the experiences that made up people's lives, both individual and social.
>
> (2016, p. 20)

Even in the construction of the interview questions, the researcher is actively involved in the inquiry process, since in creating the interview questions "the researcher becomes an integral and visible part of the research and results . . . in this way, the interview questions are as important as the participant's responses" (Raab, 2014, p. 4). In a narrative inquiry study, collaboration between the researcher and participants occurs at all levels.

Reference List

Applebaum, B. (2016, June 9). *Critical whiteness studies*. Oxford Research Encyclopedia of Education. https://oxfordre.com/education/view/10.1093/acrefore/9780190264093.001.0001/acrefore-9780190264093-e-5

Baldwin, J. (1993). *The fire next time*. Vintage International.

Baldwin, J. (2010). The white problem. In R. Kenan (Ed.), *The cross of redemption* (pp. 72–79). Pantheon Books. (Original work published 1964).

Bell, A. D. Jr. (1995a). Brown v. board of education and the interest convergence dilemma. In K. Crenshaw, N. Gotanda, G. Peller, & K. Thomas (Eds.), *Critical race theory: The key writings that formed the movement* (pp. 20–28). The New Press. (Original work 1976).

Bell, A. D. Jr. (1995b). Serving two masters: Integration ideals and the client interests in school desegregation litigation. In K. Crenshaw, N. Gotanda, G. Peller, & K. Thomas (Eds.), *Critical race theory: The key writings that formed the movement* (pp. 5–19). The New Press. (Original work published 1980).

Bonilla-Silva, E. (2001). *White supremacy and racism in the post-civil rights era*. Lynne Rienner Publishers.

Clandinin, J. D. (2016). *Engaging in narrative inquiry*. Routledge, Taylor & Francis Group.

Clandinin, J. D. & Connelly, M. F. (2000). *Narrative inquiry : experience and story in qualitative research*. Jossey-Bass Publishers

Delgado, R., & Stefancic, J. (2017). *Critical race theory: An introduction* (3rd ed.). New York University Press.

DiAngelo, R. (2016). *What does it mean to be white? Developing white racial literacy*. Peter Lang.

Du Bois, W. E. B. (1986). Criteria of negro art. In N. Huggins (Ed.), *Writings* (pp. 993–1002). The Library of America. (Original work published 1926).

Fanon, F. (2008). *Black skin, white masks*. Grove Press. (Original work published 1952).

Frankenberg, R. (1997). White women, race matters: The social construction of whiteness. In R. Delgado & J. Stefancic (Eds.), *Critical white studies: Looking behind the mirror* (pp. 632–634). Temple University Press. (Original work published 1993).

Freeman, A. D. (1995). Legitimizing racial discrimination through antidiscrimination law: A critical Review of supreme court doctrine. In Crenshaw, K., Gotanda, N., Peller, G., & Thomas, K. (Eds.), *Critical race theory: The key writings that formed the movement* (pp. 29–46). The New Press. (Original work published 1978).

Gillborn, D. (2005). Education as an act of white supremacy: Whiteness, critical race theory, and education reform. *Journal of Education Policy, 20*(4), 485–505.

Giroux, H. A. (1997). *Pedagogy and the politics of hope: Theory, culture, and schooling: A critical reader*. Westview Press.

Harris, R. (2004). Encouraging emergent moments: The personal, critical, and rhetorical in the writing classroom. *Pedagogy: Critical Approaches to Teaching Literature, Language Composition, and Culture, 4*(3), 401–418.

Helms, J. E. (1995). An update of helm's white and people of color racial identity models. In J. G. Ponterotto, J. M. Casas, L. A. Suzuki, & C. M. Alexander (Eds.), Handbook of Multicultural Counseling (p. 181–198). Sage Publications.

hooks, b. (1992). Representing whiteness in the black imagination. In L. Grossberg, C. Nelson, & P. A. Treichler (Eds.), *Cultural studies* (p. 338–346). Routledge.

Johnson, L. L. (2017). The racial Hauntings of one black male professor and the disturbance of the self(ves): Self-Actualization and racial storytelling as pedagogical practices. *Journal of Literacy Research, 49*(4), 476–502. https://doi.org/10.1177/1086296x17733779

Jupp, J. C., Berry, R. T., & Lensmire, T. J. (2016). Second-wave white teacher identity studies: A review of white teacher identity literatures from 2004 through 2014. *Review of Educational Research, 86*(4), 1151–1191. https://doi.org/10.3102/0034654316629798

Kendi, I. X. (2019). *How to be an antiracist*. One World.

Kennedy, T. M., Middleton, J. I., & Ratcliffe, K. (2005). The matter of whiteness: Or, why whiteness studies is important to rhetoric and composition. *Rhetoric Review, 24*(4), 359–373.

Ladson-Billings, G. (1998). Just what is critical race theory and what's it doing in a nice field like education? *International Journal of Qualitative Studies in Education, 11*(1), 7–24. https://doi.org/10.1080/095183998236863

Ledesma, M. C., & Calderón, D. (2015). Critical race theory in education. *Qualitative Inquiry, 21*(3), 206–222. https://doi.org/10.1177/1077800414557825

Lensmire, T., Mcmanimon, S., Tierney, J. D., Lee-Nichols, M., Casey, Z., Lensmire, A., & Davis, B. (2013). McIntosh as synecdoche: How teacher education's focus on white privilege undermines antiracism. Harvard Educational Review, 83(3), 410–431. https://doi.org/10.17763/haer.83.3.35054h1418230574

Leonardo, Z. (2009). *Race, whiteness, and education*. Routledge.

Levine-Rasky, C. (2000) The practice of whiteness among teacher candidates. International Studies in Sociology of Education, 10(3), 263-284. https://doi.org/10.1080/09620210000200060

Lynch, I., Swartz, S., & Isaacs, D. (2017). Anti-racist moral education: A review of approaches, impact and theoretical underpinnings from 2000 to 2015. Journal of Moral Education, 46(2), 129–144. https://doi.org/10.1080/03057240.2016.1273825

McIntosh, P. (1997). White privilege and male privilege: A personal account of coming to see correspondences through work in women's studies. In R. Delgado & J. Stefancic (Eds.), *Critical white studies: Looking behind the mirror* (pp. 291–299). Temple University Press. (Original work published 1988).

Michael, A. (2015). *Raising race questions: Whiteness and inquiry in education*. Teachers College Press

Mills, C. W. (1997). *The racial contract*. Cornell University Press.

Morrison, T. (1992). Playing in the dark: whiteness and the literary imagination. Vintage Books.

Picower, B. (2009). The unexamined Whiteness of teaching: how White teachers maintain and enact dominant racial ideologies. Race Ethnicity and Education, 12(2), 197–215. https://doi.org/10.1080/13613320902995475

Raab, D. (2014). Creative transcendence: Memoir writing for transformation and empowerment. *The Journal of Transpersonal Psychology, 46*(2), 1–21.

Roediger, D. (1991). *The wages of Whiteness*. Verso.

Tanner, S. J. (2019). Whiteness is a white problem: Whiteness in English education. *English Education, 51*(2), 182–198.

Watson, V. T. (2013). *The souls of white folk: African American writers theorize whiteness*. University Press of Mississippi.

Yagelski, R. P. (2009). A thousand writers writing: Seeking change through the radical practice of writing as a way of being. *English Education, 42*(1), 6–28.

3 The Study

Alex and Anna's Racially Reflective Journey

In this chapter I discuss the research design and methodological practices that were required to address the research questions related to the puzzle of practice. I begin by discussing narrative inquiry, the methodology I utilized to tell the story of my participants in this study. I also highlight the connection between narrative inquiry and action research. As discussed in Chapter 2, writing can translate to a way of being. This change is at the heart of action research. I then go on to discuss the setting of the study, the participants of the study, my data collection and analysis procedures, my role as the researcher in the study, the validity of the data, the limitations of the research design, and any ethical concerns in the research design.

The Connection Between Narrative Inquiry Action Research

The research design of this study was in the tradition of narrative inquiry. This methodology made the most sense for my study because of its inherent fluidity. Narrative inquiry is "not a set of procedures or linear steps to be followed but a relational inquiry methodology that is open to where the stories of participants' experience take each researcher" (Clandenin, 2016, p. 33). At the core of my study were the acts of "living, telling, retelling, and reliving" (p. 34). My participants told their personal and professional stories of White racial identity. They retold these stories (and told new ones) in our race inquiry group meetings. They told the story of their lived experience of being in the race inquiry group and the story of how being in the group affected how they relived their experiences personally and professionally. They told the story of how the act of writing personal narratives impacted the development of their racial identity and racial competency. Lastly, I told the story of the totality of the experiences of my participants throughout the course of my study. In light of the multitude of directions these stories could have gone, narrative inquiry was the most appropriate methodological model for my study.

However, this study also aimed to assess the degree to which engaging in the study motivated the participants to create change in their personal lives, in their classrooms, or in their school. In this, I see the research design of narrative inquiry as a means to engage in action research as well. The telling and retelling of the stories of one's life as part of the narrative inquiry process can indeed lead to real change. Clandinin et al. (2007) discuss the interconnectedness between narrative inquiry and action research, saying:

> These ideas of story living and telling, retelling and reliving are central features in [Clandinin and Connelly's], and our particular view of narrative inquiry. For them, the inquiry into narrative, stories lived and told, creates spaces, gaps, which allow for change. Within their conceptualization, there are clear connections between narrative inquiry and a broad view of action research.
>
> (p. 292)

While I recognize the dominant research design of this study was that of narrative inquiry, I also cannot deny the connection between the stories my participants told as part of the narrative inquiry process and the actionable change that can come from engaging in this self-inquiry.

Setting

The setting of my study was my place of work. The school is a charter high school for the arts located in eastern Pennsylvania. The students at the school are predominantly White (66.7% of the population), and the teachers are almost exclusively White. Of the students, 8.8% are Black, 13.7% are Hispanic, and 8.2% identify as being multiracial. Furthermore, 33.4% of the students are categorized as economically disadvantaged (PA Future Ready Index, 2018). In many ways, the school is a reflection of America: a White-dominated setting where somehow whiteness and its effects remain almost invisible.

Description of Participants

All participants signed a consent form that outlined their details and expectations for the study. I recruited two White participants for my study because the focus of my study was on how White teachers process the ways in which their whiteness contextualizes their personal and professional worldviews. While this was a small sample, the participants were chosen very carefully. I wanted to capture as many variables as possible in my chosen participants as they related to gender and their content area.

1. Alex is a male core discipline teacher who taught at the school for seven years. He was a new father at the time of this study. He cited always being willing to learn more about the implications of his racial identity.

2. Anna is a female arts discipline instructor who taught at the school for 16 years. She taught in multiple capacities throughout the course of her career, including collegiately and in private settings. She is a mother of three who describes herself as the most racially aware member of her department at the school. She also cited having a willingness to learn more about the implications of her racial identity.

I primarily chose these two participants in order to have a male and female perspective and because one teaches a core discipline subject and the other teaches an artistic discipline at the school. I also chose both participants because they expressed an interest in doing this kind of White racial inquiry work and are veteran teachers. Both participants saw themselves as educators who were aware of racial issues in the classroom and who felt they had done work to make their classrooms more equitable.

Data Collection Procedures

Seeing as this was a case study of the experiences of teachers engaging in narrative racial inquiry and the goal was to create thick descriptions of participant experience gathered from multiple in-depth data sources, I kept my number of participants rather low. The bulk of my data was gathered from the writings of my participants as well as my observations and interviews with them.

The rationale behind using multiple methods to collect data was to gauge how the various methods interact/build off one another and to uncover what realizations of my participants come by engaging in each respective context (alone in their writing, in a group setting, one-on-one with me at the end of the study). What results were unique to my participants engaging in these questions about race alone in their writings? What results were unique to my participants working through these questions together as they discussed their writings? What results were unique to my participants having the opportunity to look back on their experiences in the study as a whole and reflect on them via the exit interview? For example, what they articulated in the first section of their personal narratives and first meeting may not have represented their feelings after completing the study in full. They may have come to more multifaceted/detailed/complex conclusions that they could not come to earlier in the study. The exit interview allowed the opportunity for my participants to tell the stories of their experience in the study in full after all of the writings and meetings were completed.

While the questions I mention above do not necessarily represent my primary research questions, they are questions I was able to speak to in the results and discussion portion of the study by utilizing various data collection methods. Through collecting data in multiple ways, I was able to better speak to any growth/transformation/shifting of ideologies that occurred in my participants by the end of the study, as well as the specific environments from which these transformative moments were born. Another reason for utilizing these three data collection methods was the potential to validate data through triangulation. While the different collection methods might have offered different results depending on the method utilized, I was also able to speak to the similar patterns I observed in the data across the three data sources via triangulation.

Personal Narratives

I asked my participants to write in-depth personal narratives that consisted of four primary sections. I offered participants some writing prompts to consider in order to ground their writing in specific details. I summarize these sections below. These sections correlated strongly with the research questions listed in Chapter 1.

1. **How has my racial identity affected/contextualized my experiences on a personal level?** In this section, participants recounted memories from their lives that affected the degree to which they became aware of their racial identity. They discussed why they chose to refer to these memories and how they affected their personal worldviews moving forward regarding race and how being White impacts them and the lives of others.
2. **How has my racial identity affected/contextualized my experiences on a professional level as a teacher?** In this section, participants connected these personal epiphanies regarding their racial identity to their experiences in the classroom. How is the education system dominated by whiteness? How does being White affect the way they teach? How does being White affect the way they interact with their students? How do they think being White affects the way their students respond to them? Do they think being White affects any of these things at all?
3. **How can I employ more holistic antiracist pedagogies?** In this section, participants described ways they sought not only to speak to White privilege in their classrooms but also ways to challenge the White-dominated systems in place that allow for these privileges in the first place. How will they make whiteness visible in their classrooms? How will they challenge their White students to speak to race to the same degree they expect their students of color to speak to race in the classroom?
4. **How did reflecting on my racial identity through writing and discussion impact me personally and professionally?** In this final section, participants discussed how they were impacted by the experience of reflecting on their racial identity and discussing these reflections with colleagues in our meetings after the writing of each section. Did they have any epiphanies in doing this work? Did they find anything that surprised them? Did the experience

change the way they saw themselves in relation to the world around them? Did the experience change the way they thought about their role(s) in the classroom? Was there anything specific to the act of writing that aided in their racial identity development?

The writing of this personal narrative was scaffolded so that participants engaged with only one section at a time. Participants were given each section of the personal narrative at the beginning of the month and had three weeks to draft each section. I then took a few days to read that particular section of each participant prior to our group meetings.

Race Inquiry Group Meetings

Participants then met with me as a group in the final week of the month to discuss their writing experiences and what they discovered. We met for anywhere between 40 minutes and an hour, depending on how the conversation was unfolding. These group meetings were more conversational and less structured. Though the conversation flowed freely, we asked the same two questions as part of every group meeting:

1. What was your overall experience in writing this section?
2. Were there any specific epiphanies you came to in writing this section that you would like to share?

The purpose of holding these meetings was twofold. First, it gave participants the opportunity to expand on the thoughts they articulated in their narratives. Second, it created an environment that functioned as a community of writers and antiracist practitioners. In allowing the participants to recount their stories together and share ideas, I wanted to observe the degree to which the group came to further develop a sense of shared goals and responsibilities as antiracist educators. I was interested to see how my participants articulated how the group meetings that occurred after drafting each section of their personal narratives impacted their subsequent writings and reflections.

Exit Interviews

I also performed an exit interview with each participant individually, as this one-on-one context provided more data regarding how the participants characterized their experience in the study and what personal and professional revelations they came to. These exit interviews were fully structured, where all participants responded to the same set of questions. I met virtually with each participant for roughly 15 minutes each to conduct these interviews.

Data Analysis Procedures

Each of my research questions was embedded in the sections of the personal narratives that I asked my participants to write. Each conversation allowed for further exploration of my research questions. In this way, I used inductive coding to code my participant responses for each section of their narrative. I also used inductive coding to organize my observation data and the exit interview data. Based on the coding of these responses from the written narratives, group meetings, and interviews, I identified themes that helped provide thick descriptions that characterized the degree to which my participants believed their whiteness impacts them personally and professionally. I also aimed to provide thick descriptions that characterized the degree to which my participants felt the process of writing personal narratives and engaging in open discourse about their whiteness impacts them personally and professionally.

Researcher Role

While the group meetings were facilitated by me, I was mainly there to observe and take notes on how the conversations unfolded. In an attempt to stay as neutral as possible, I began each meeting by asking, "Are there any specific epiphanies or realizations that you would like to mention that stemmed from your writing?" It was my participants' writing itself that best protected the study from biased results. While I did give the participants various possible writing prompts, I did not tell them they were required to write about anything. I did not begin by telling them, "your racial identity undoubtedly impacts you and the world around you, so now begin writing." It was their choice as to the direction they took their writing. And since their conversations were based on what they wrote prior to my involvement with them in the meetings, I played little part in affecting any of the results. It is true that new data was collected from the transcripts during these meetings. But again, this data came from the building off and expansion of ideas they had already written about in their narratives and were simply fleshed out in more detail through our group conversations. I paid close attention to avoid guiding my participants in any specific direction during their discussions. I allowed the conversations to unfold between the two of them as I took notes on the various directions they took the conversation. However, I did share experiences of my own to create a deep sense of trust and community within the group.

Reference List

Clandinin, D. J., Pushor, D., & Orr, A. M. (2007). Navigating sites for narrative inquiry. *Journal of Teacher Education, 58*(1).

Clandinin. J. D. (2016). Engaging in narrative inquiry. Routledge, Taylor & Francis Group

Future ready PA index - school fast facts - lehigh valley charter high school for the arts. (2018). Futurereadypa.org. https://futurereadypa.org/School/FastFacts?id=0510580690 5510311625200003720017005910318 6146032

4 Whiteness as a Barrier to Developing Racial Competency in One's Personal Life

This theme consisted of the ways that my participants described various aspects of whiteness and how they acted as barriers to the development of their racial competency throughout the course of their personal lives. While I did not directly ask them to discuss barriers to developing their racial competency, this is a theme that developed from what they shared in their writing and conversations. Overall, this theme is characterized by an asserted general lack of awareness on the part of my participants in regard to their racial identity, a lack of awareness largely the result of being White.

Lack of Awareness

Throughout the course of the study, and regardless of the particular section my participants were working on in their personal narrative, they consistently referenced a general lack of awareness regarding their racial identity and issues of race as a result of being White. Alex wrote, "the question of race is about as scarce as a rain cloud in the Sahara. Today I recognize my young life as one of distinct privilege: my lack of any awareness of race as a construct or issue was a gift given by my skin." More specifically relating to education, Alex wrote:

> Because the ride was made for me, I was oblivious to this until recently. The fact that I was oblivious while others desperately tried to fit into 'white schooling' furthers the point that our system from the foundation is built to keep white people in power and whitewash all else.

Anna mentioned, "Because of my whiteness, I have never had to worry about the daily oppression of racism in my home country and while traveling in the places that I went to." She also cited what she deemed to be the biggest mistake of her early teaching career. She said, "The biggest mistake I made as a young teacher was thinking race was irrelevant." It is clear through these representative statements that lacking an awareness of their own racial identity negatively impacted my participants' ability to develop racial competency in their personal lives.

DOI: 10.4324/9781032659305-5

While they do not explicitly speak to a lack of awareness being a barrier, it goes without saying that being unaware of something does not allow one to address it. In this way, being generally unaware of their racial identity acted as a barrier to developing a deeper understanding of the implications of this racial identity.

Public Racial Life versus Private Racial Life

The tension between the public racial lives and private racial lives of my participants and their families also impacted the degree to which my participants were able to develop racial competency throughout the course of their lives. Anna discussed at length the discrepancy between her parents' professional lives and personal lives regarding race. She said:

> No matter what job I held over the years at the hospital, one recurring theme that came up was that my mom was the "nice administrator" who always helped people. She didn't bring up race for the most part in all the years we worked there together. However, in her time working in maternal child health, there were abandoned babies that she always talked about wanting to adopt. She always exclaimed how adorable the "chocolate" babies were and how she wanted to bring them home to give them a better life. I'm not sure if she was serious but she often repeated how "cute the babies that black people made" were. Unknowingly and unintended, I believe now that this was a form of "positive racism" where one implies that all members of a group have some positive characteristic . . . I do remember that if my dad had been drinking alcoholic beverages, he would occasionally say the phrase 'Black is beautiful, tan is grand but white is the color of American' which my mom would scold him for (with a smile on her face) and every time he would say it, I would remark to him how inappropriate it was but I would also giggle . . . I remember really being confused by her comment because my always seemed ok with people of different colors and races. Not only that, she was usually their advocate . . . I feel like there is such a two-faced thing with everything . . . there was such a double standard in my parents.

Anna went on to say that witnessing her parents act in racist ways in private made her do the same at times, particularly with her groups of White friends. She said:

> I am ashamed to admit that I also remember telling racist jokes myself. I feel guilty even typing about the jokes I told . . . my White majority friend group was completely comfortable contributing to the oppression of another through our jokes. It didn't even cross our minds that it was wrong.

Alex echoed these sentiments regarding the telling of racist jokes, saying:

> How many of those jokes were made in the company of White people? And unfortunately, whether it was a joke about being gay or being Black or whatever, those jokes were made consistently in a group of friends where you felt safe and comfortable making those jokes.

This push and pull between their private and public racial lives negatively impacted my participants' ability to develop a positive racial identity and build their racial competency.

Barriers to Developing Racial Competency

The belief that they were "not racist" negatively impacted Alex and Anna's ability to process their racial identity and develop a stronger racial competency. While growing up, Alex recounted feeling:

> "I'm fairly positive I'm not a racist so I don't have to do anything else. Like I already knew where I was and that was it . . . I think about my experiences in college and I was like I like hip hop music and hip-hop culture. I voted for Barack Obama. I can't be racist. It was like all these things I was like putting it in my mind that were reasons why I'm doing enough and it was never enough.

While Alex tied his "not racist" persona to having friends of color and engaging with what he deemed to be the culture of people of color, Anna believed she could not be racist because of being in a romantic relationship with a person of color earlier in her life. She stated, "I'm not racist because I've loved someone who's not White." Believing that they were not racist created an obstacle for my participants to more fully see how their racial identity functioned in their personal world and in the world around them in more subtle and nuanced ways.

Impact of Their Upbringing

My participants discussed the degree to which the way they were raised impacted their beliefs about race. These beliefs made it difficult for them to process their racial identity in more complex ways. Alex said, "I had ingrained beliefs, but I never had to actively use them. It was a textbook topic, not something I confronted daily." Anna discussed the difficulty of trying to rid herself of dangerous racial stereotypes that were taught to her throughout her upbringing. She said, "I don't know if this is from my upbringing, but I became aware that I had a tendency to make racializations throughout my life and I have to work hard to get away from those stereotypes when they pop into my brain." Being raised to think about race in a certain way (or not at all) impeded Alex and Anna's ability to further identify what being White meant to them and the people around them.

Growing Up in White Communities

According to Alex and Anna, growing up in predominantly White communities negatively impacted their ability to process their racial identity. Anna wrote:

> My entire neighborhood was White, my school was predominately White, all of my friends were White, everyone in my dance class was White and everyone I associated with was White. I'm sure I must have seen people of color outside of my mom's work, but they were so scarce and not anyone I knew so I have no memory of being aware of race in my younger years except for my time spent at the hospital.

Alex said, "I think it's also important to note I grew up in White suburbia. Safe, clean, unrestricted . . . my entire life has been like this cocoon of suburbia and it sheltered me from all the issues around race." Growing up in predominantly White communities made invisible to Alex and Anna the greater complexities and implications of being White.

Whiteness as Protection

Both Alex and Anna spoke to the notion that being White provided them protection from negative circumstances, particularly with police officers. Alex recounted being in the car when his wife was pulled over by a police officer. He remembered:

> He's like this is just a warning, this isn't anything, don't worry about it. Just please drive the speed limit, get home safe, good luck with your child is coming. That's my experience with the police my entire life. And that's not fair. And the other thing is, I've made it a point over the last two or three years when I see anyone pulled over, I look to see who they are. Are they Black? Are they a minority in some way shape or form? And it's got to be 75% minority. And that's just my personal experience of seeing it, and it's a constant reminder of the privilege I enjoy.

Anna recounted an even more shocking story where she put her hands on an officer. She said, "I slapped a police officer in the face and said cuff me, I've been a bad girl. I mean what would that have been like if I wasn't a White girl?" Going through life dodging negative outcomes just on the basis of being White kept the implications of their racial identity hidden.

5 Whiteness as a Barrier to Creating Antiracist Educational Spaces

The following themes and sub-themes were identified from the data sources in relation to my second research question: How does writing personal narratives about race impact how White teachers process how their whiteness affects their professional experiences in the classroom? This research question focused on how my participants reflected on the implications of their race in their professional lives and how they have processed their racial identity in relation to their role as a teacher throughout the course of their professional careers.

Whiteness as a Barrier to Developing Racial Competency in Relation to Education

After reflecting on their own experiences in school and as educators, both Alex and Anna came to see whiteness as a barrier to their ability to develop racial competency, specifically as it relates to education. The sub-themes out of this more overarching theme speak to my participants' belief that the blanket of whiteness that shrouds American education did not allow them to develop a positive racial competency as it related to their schooling and their role as an educator.

Experiences as a White Student

Alex and Anna discussed how being White in school made it difficult for them to see any connection between whiteness and education. Anna wrote:

> I have the privilege of being fearless because I have never had to experience discrimination in the classroom because of my race. I didn't realize what challenges my students of color had to negotiate in predominantly White academic environments. My students of color have no choice but to think about and understand race on a daily basis and it was my white privilege that kept me from seeing this for so long.

Alex said:

> Through my own education both in primary and secondary school, I never needed to reckon with my whiteness because being White meant I was the baseline, I was the neutral. So from my point of view, being White did not affect the way I learned or the way I teach. I didn't ever need to address my whiteness because it was a net zero from my perspective. In fact, as a White man, I have never in my life experienced a feeling of otherness.

Seeing whiteness as the baseline for normalcy in school did not allow Alex and Anna to develop racial competency as it related to their education.

Whiteness as the Educational Standard

Alex and Anna spoke to how the education system being structured in a way that positions whiteness as the educational standard has impacted their ability to develop their racial competency as it relates to schooling. Anna wrote:

> Whiteness dictates the standard to which all other behaviors are evaluated. . . . It's very discouraging to work in an environment where whiteness and Western norms are so heavily valued and anything else is strongly resisted and even made fun of at times.

Alex further elaborated on Anna's point writing:

> Education is a vast historical construct of classism and racism. It has been structured in a way to establish whiteness as the baseline, "the normal," and thus also establish anyone else as an "other." Its design allows the maintaining of the status quo. We don't teach history, we teach white history. We don't teach English, we teach white English. We don't teach health, we teach white health. If you are not white, you are simply a passenger on a ride not made for you. Whiteness is a slow, thick mist that strangles everyone in education and attempts to fit all colors, shapes, and forms into its single box. It lays over education like a malaise of complacency lulling White educators and students into the false belief that whiteness is average and not different.

Spending their time learning and teaching in a way that makes whiteness the "norm" of education negatively impacted Alex and Anna's ability to see their racial identity as having any impact on the way they were schooled or how they educated their students.

Feelings of Not Doing Enough

This overarching theme consists of my participants' feelings of not doing enough to address their whiteness and/or racism in their school and/or classrooms and the reasons for not going further in developing this racial competency as it relates to their school/classrooms. These feelings of not doing enough created a general lack of motivation to further develop their racial competency. The sub-themes that follow highlight these more specific feelings related to not doing enough to address their whiteness and/or combat racism in their school and/or classrooms and the more specific reasons for not doing more on these fronts.

Passivity

Alex and Anna recounted times in their professional careers as educators where they felt they were too passive in addressing their whiteness and/or racial issues in their classroom. Alex wrote:

> I presented myself as an ally, a compassionate sympathizer, but I did not recognize my own whiteness was actually a barrier to many of my students. I think what scares me more than anything is to think that I have contributed to the damaging mindset that whiteness is normal and all else because of my lack of awareness . . . I am angry but more than that I am sad. I am angry I worked in silence perpetuating a lie of white normality for so long. I am sad that I probably hurt students without knowing along the way . . . my complicity throughout my life in keeping Whites in power frustrates me to my core.

Anna commented:

> The more I talk about it, the more embarrassed I am that it is this way and that I haven't fought harder for a collective acknowledgement of this issue. . . . While I do feel I am far ahead of my peers in my diversity work, I have fallen short by only fighting small battles, by being inconsistent, by drawing a line when things get too uncomfortable and by staying silent when I should've spoken up.

These feelings of anger, frustration, embarrassment, guilt, and regret that came as a result of Alex and Anna's passivity in the face of racial issues pushed them away from developing their racial competency.

Discouragement

Feeling discouraged further impacted Alex and Anna's willingness to do more in the face of whiteness and/or racism. Alex talked about the size and complexity of the problem when he said, "The problem is so vast, and it is hard not to feel powerless." Where Alex's feeling of discouragement came from the vastness of the problem, Anna's came from the unwillingness of her peers to see the problem at all. She wrote:

> I wish my peers would take time rooting out their biases and be encouraged to make changes but if I'm being honest, the last 16 years haven't given me much hope that they will . . . I am working hard to use this as motivation to be encouraged to do more instead of discouraged because it's so challenging.

Feeling discouraged left Alex and Anna unmotivated to do the work necessary to develop their racial competency so that they could better navigate issues of whiteness and/or racism in their school and/or classroom.

Fear of Social Repercussions

A fear of social repercussions regarding the addressing of whiteness and/or racism resulted in both Alex and Anna feeling like they did not do enough. Anna remembered an experience she had with a good friend and colleague that shook her. She said:

> I remember being in our school's theater after one of our performances started. A Black family came into the audience late after the show had started. As they were finding their seats, one of my dearest friends/dance teacher peers turned to me and said 'they're on colored people time.' I could feel the blood rushing into my cheeks. I was speechless, yet I am ashamed to say I just got quiet. It was an opportunity for me to call her out on her racist comment, yet I didn't. How is it that after all the work I have done to improve my racial awareness, I still struggle to speak up and face my peers when they say something racist?

Alex spoke more generally, saying that "I don't want to get so afraid of ramifications that may or may not exist that I don't fully commit to being an ally and an agent of change." Both participants discussed a fear of the social repercussions that kept them from engaging with racial issues in a way that may have further developed their racial competency.

Ineffective Prior Professional Development Trainings

Alex and Anna discussed the ineffectiveness of prior professional development training as a reason for not doing enough in their school/classroom in relation to addressing whiteness and/or racism. Anna talked specifically about the ineffectiveness of the large group setting for professional development training. She said, "So I would say the antiracist work I've done in the past has probably been myself in a group of 10 to 60 people. And what I realized is you're not as accountable that way." Alex said:

> And I think that for me has made [the study] so much more valuable than anything else I've done any training I've had at school, whether it's in a group setting or something I have to, you know, a video I have to watch whatever . . . that all just scratches such a big surface . . . I don't think enough of that work was real, was honest, was scary.

Both Alex and Anna saw ineffective professional development training as deterrents from doing more critical racial competency work.

6 Combatting the Whiteness of Education Through Teacher Development and Through Classroom Instruction

The following themes and sub-themes were identified from the data sources in relation to my third research question: How does writing personal narratives about race affect the ability of White teachers to develop more holistic antiracist pedagogies? This research question focused on how my participants discussed ways they planned to implement more authentically antiracist practices in their classrooms after having reflected on the implications of their racial identity personally and professionally in the prior two sections of their narratives.

Combatting the Whiteness of Education Through Teacher Development

Alex and Anna's responses regarding the ways they thought they could create more authentically antiracist classrooms fell into two major themes. This first theme consisted of their responses that included what they thought could be done in the way of teacher development to prepare the teacher to create a more authentically antiracist classroom.

Importance of Deep Critical Self-reflection

Alex and Anna spoke at length about the integral role they felt that critical self-reflection plays in a teacher's ability to develop racial competency and thus better lead an antiracist classroom. Anna discussed not being given the opportunity to do deep reflection in prior professional development training, saying, "And so, in a way I think part of the reason why I brushed off aspects of it was because we weren't digging deep enough into it and it wasn't personal and I didn't care." Alex echoed these sentiments saying:

> But I don't think that they help us reflect enough . . . this process of looking back, looking at my experience today and then looking at the future really helped to build my perspective on what it means to be an antiracist teacher and what that means in a school.

Importance of Small Group Discussions

Connected to the necessity for deep reflection that Alex and Anna discussed, they also spoke to the benefit of reflecting on their racial identity and other issues of race in a small group setting. Anna said:

> And I think in this small setting where we had this opportunity to do this with the three of us is really helpful because the only work that we've done before on this at our job has been in a huge group setting where we break away in small groups. But they're not that small, and it's not the exploratory work, you know, maybe 20% of the depth of what of the hundred percent we're doing here.

Alex too mentioned the benefit of engaging in small group discussions, saying, "I think that we would benefit a lot more from this kind of smaller scale reflective practice of thinking about okay, well, how has my whiteness impacted things?"

Creating Actionable Items

Alex and Anna discussed the usefulness of creating a list of actionable items or daily reminders to keep themselves honest as antiracist educators. Anna included the list of Peggy McIntosh's (1988) knapsack of White privileges. She found this list while doing her own research outside of our inquiry group and said that it is something accessible that she could look at to check her White privilege in the classroom. Alex made his own list of actionable items, saying:

> I found myself trying to create really actionable items. Because I think, in a lot of my writing so far, I tend to lean towards more like ideological stuff and like it's these broad statements of like I need to do better, but it's never actionable. So what I found myself leaning towards this time was what can I actually do, like, day to day, minute to minute to be actively antiracist to support my students of all shapes and sizes and colors.

Combatting the Whiteness of Education in the Classroom

While in the theme described above Alex and Anna discussed what they felt could be done in the way of teacher development to prepare teachers to create more authentically antiracist classrooms, their responses that make up this following theme consist of the strategies they planned to implement in their own classrooms in order to foster an antiracist learning environment.

Building Relationships/Creating Community

Alex and Anna noted how integral it is to build meaningful relationships with their students and build a sense of community in the classroom in order to create an antiracist classroom. Alex discussed the importance of being honest with his students about issues of race as part of building meaningful relationships with his students. Alex said:

> I know I can be an agent for real change and understanding, and I can start by being honest in my classroom about my own whiteness and all the things I don't know. If nothing else, my eyes have been opened to what I don't know and what I have taken for granted. That knowledge or lack thereof is invaluable to becoming a true antiracist teacher.

Anna mentioned the critical nature of building a classroom community, stating, "As mentioned in the above lesson plan, identity charts can 'build relationships, break down stereotypes, and start to build classroom community.' I feel this will really help me evolve into the teacher I need to be in TODAY'S world."

Giving Students Opportunities to Discuss Race

Alex and Anna discussed the importance of offering students opportunities to discuss race in the classroom. Alex wrote:

> I want to make sure that my students of all races are aware of the historical construction and limitations of the education system. I want to provide them with knowledge and tools to address and overcome the shortcomings of the education system as it has been constructed.

Alex went on to discuss how he needs to offer more opportunities to discuss race in the classroom that go beyond the surface. He went on to say:

> Over the last couple of years my passivity towards racial topics has been brought to my attention. In front of my students, I would address topics, I would describe things as "messed up" or "wrong," but I wouldn't push further or ask my students to take into account their own experiences or race. I figured being a conscientious ally would be enough to show my Black students I understood and my White students what they should care about. That was never enough, and I have done a disservice to all of my students by thinking this way.

Anna discussed ways to offer these opportunities through the discipline of dance, saying:

> I imagine them watching all of the movement projects that each group comes up with. This would lend itself to important conversations and multifaceted expression amongst my students. It will also help them feel more

comfortable expressing similar emotions that may come up for them in their daily experiences.

She went on further to discuss the importance of giving students the power in the classroom to address issues of race, saying, "In addition to teachers, the students should have the power to address bias and racism in the dance studio."

Reference List

McIntosh, P. (1997). White privilege and male privilege: A personal account of coming to see correspondences through work in women's studies. In Delgado, R. & Stefancic, J. (Eds.), Critical white studies: Looking behind the mirror (pp. 291-299). Temple University Press. (Original work published 1988)

7 Writing as a Way of Seeing and Being

The following themes and sub-themes were identified from the data sources in relation to my fourth research question: How does participating in group meetings rooted in the discussion of their personal narratives about race impact the way White teachers process their whiteness personally and professionally? This research question focused on how my participants discussed the degree to which the act of writing impacted their ability to process their racial identity and its implications in various areas of their lives.

Writing as a Way of Seeing and Being

This theme speaks to the many ways that Alex and Anna saw writing as a powerful tool to strengthen their racial competency. The sub-themes of this larger theme highlight the myriad of ways that Alex and Anna believed deep reflective writing helped them to find a higher sense of seeing and being in regard to their racial identity.

Increased Awareness

Alex and Anna discussed a general increase in awareness regarding the impact of their racial identity through the act of writing. Alex said:

> My ability wasn't there, because I wasn't aware. My awareness of my own racial identity didn't exist in a lot of ways . . . part of this experience for me has been really for the first time in my life grappling with my own racial identity. For me, understanding that I have my own racial makeup and, and then mindset to overcome and to think about and to always take into account. That was the biggest breakthrough, maybe of this entire thing for me.

Anna said, "And it also brought an awareness, personally, professionally and generally to how big the problem is and how important it is to do something about it."

Depth of Understanding

Perhaps above all else, Alex and Anna cited coming to a deeper understanding of their racial identity and its impact on them and the people around them through the act of writing. Anna said, "As a result of our intimate group setting and writing in depth about race in all aspects of my life, I now understand my personal and professional relationship with race on a deeper level and am therefore able to make more substantial strides in tackling racial equity issues in my personal and professional life." Alex elaborated on Anna's thoughts, saying:

> The discussions and reflections I have taken part in through this have helped me dig past my "I'm not a racist" surface mindset as well as my white passivity and privilege . . . I started this process as a passive-minded faux antiracist who had read some books and started to tweak the things I teach. I needed to sit down and get in my feelings through reflection and conversation in order to understand the scope of my own relationship with race and my own whiteness.

Anna spoke to getting beyond the surface that Alex referenced above when she said,

> but when I started writing them all down. And then one would spark. Oh yeah, this happened. And that happened I was like, I didn't even get to some of the things that sparked me to write about, but I was like amazed by how much there was and so it really, you know, I knew racism is an issue in the world, and other places, and maybe I thought in the institution I work at like there's things, but I guess I didn't realize how prevalent it was or didn't want to realize how prevalent it was in my life . . . so, that in addition to being able to explore it more deeper than I ever have in the past. I also realize the power.

Alex spoke to this depth of experience, further saying:

> And I think this process of writing down and really combing through my mind of my experiences with race has gotten me to a different level of understanding. It has allowed me to be honest in a way that I'm not normally honest. . . . So, the act of writing in this kind of long form allowed me to be honest, and I think I called it at some points a reckoning like I was able to really grapple with my own feelings on race, my own thoughts on race and really think about how much I don't think about race when I should.

Writing Created a Sense of Permanence/Reality

Alex and Anna spoke to how the act of writing created a sense of permanence that offered them more clarity in terms of seeing how their racial identity impacts themselves and the people around them. Anna said:

> I think that things when they exist in your heart, emotions and in your head, no one has to know about them, if that makes sense or like, they can always live there in that safe zone. But it's more of like a literal existing thing when I take those thoughts out of my psyche and put them on paper, or in a computer, or like it makes it something that is real and brought into my conscious mind and not just, you know, only in my individual body, if that makes sense. So, I mean, it's in a way, it's like it's almost like I have all those thoughts and realizations in my hand. You know, like holding it. And it's not just floating around in there and never dissected. Like I never tried to understand it. So, by taking it out, it helps me. It informs me in a way it wouldn't have informed me. I think the biggest epiphany personally for me was that I'm sure I knew I had some work to do. But I didn't realize the extent of work for me on a personal level on a professional level but just generally how much the how much work there still is to do . . . it made it real for me.

Alex too spoke to the feeling that writing made his realizations more concrete. He said:

> It makes me think about how many epiphanies I've had over the course of my life. And I've had so many. But the difference between most of them and a couple of them is making them real, because I have these fleeting epiphanies that I'm like, I understand something for a moment and then if I haven't written it down or done something with it, it goes away and if you ask me in a day or a week or whatever, I won't remember that epiphany. This process helped me to make concrete many epiphanies about race that normally would have been fleeting thoughts. And, you know, that has to make me a better person, a better educator and help me and my students and anyone else . . . I'll have these, these moments of clarity. But a lot of the problem for me is remembering them. A lot of them happen. I have this beautiful moment of clarity and then it fades away. So the act of writing for me makes things a little more permanent. It allows me to slow things down and really go over the ideas and make that breakthrough that can be more permanent, so I don't just have that thought and then it fades away and then like two days later and like I had a really good thought on this topic but it's gone now. No, I feel really confident that these changes that I'm making in my mindset. And my understanding of race and whiteness are far more permanent because of the writing process.

Writing as a Way of Seeing and Being 53

Writing as a Tool of Accountability

Alex and Anna discussed how the act of writing and seeing their thoughts on paper made them feel like they needed to hold themselves more accountable in regard to their racial identity and other issues of race in their personal and professional lives. Alex said, "And I think this process has allowed me to see actual methods for accountability that I don't just have . . . I shouldn't just cruise and assume that I'm doing enough." Anna spoke to the overwhelming feeling that came with reading all of the issues of race that surround her saying:

> But then, like kind of this epiphany of being like, okay, all these things are happening professionally around me and by not speaking up I'm just part of the problem. And I have to do some work to figure out how I can, you know, be more inclined to speak up, be braver to speak up, and more equipped to speak up.

Writing as a Tool to Organize Thoughts

Alex and Anna talked about how writing gave them a structure to organize their thoughts. Anna said:

> The act of writing in this case, brought these occurrences to the forefront of my mind and organized my thoughts and feelings in a way that I am now able to better use them to inform my life in the future. You know, and it organized my thoughts in a way to understand the whole picture. I understood bits and pieces of it before but I didn't realize.

While Alex never mentioned the word "organization specifically," he too spoke to the general notion that writing allowed him to see a fuller picture that he would not have otherwise seen. He said, "And I got to, you know, write it down and edit it and then go over it and like what am I missing. And that, that's just it's such a different process."

Writing as Empowerment/Motivated to Action

Alex and Anna both discussed feeling empowered and motivated to action through the act of writing. Alex said:

> I feel so empowered by this process. I'm at the point where I don't want to write anymore. I want to enact change in my classroom, school, and life. I know I can be an agent for real change and understanding, and I can start by being honest in my classroom about my own whiteness and all the things I don't know. If nothing else, my eyes have been opened to what I don't know

and what I have taken for granted. That knowledge or lack thereof is invaluable to becoming a true antiracist teacher.

Anna spoke to not only feeling more motivated and empowered to act through the process of writing, but she also spoke to how she feels more prepared to address issues of race in her personal and professional life. She said:

> I also feel I am more prepared and more motivated to speak up in ways I have been unable to do in the past. From all my soul searching, research and the work that these writings allowed me to do, the importance of doing right by every person really revealed itself to me and inspires me to do better. Just because I am not directly harmed by racism, I truly understand the importance of fighting for those that are. I still have so much to learn and so much more to do but I am so thankful for the insight and tools this experience has given me. I feel so much more prepared and inspired to actively take a stand against racism.

Benefits of Small Group Discussions

Alex and Anna spoke to the benefits of discussing their writing in small groups. Alex spoke to the value of hearing other people's perspectives, saying:

> The beauty of the discussion aspect of it was hearing that secondary perspective on the same topic opened up doors in my mind that were forgotten that I had no idea. I could connect different things. Until, Anna would talk about something and all of a sudden a light bulb again. These epiphany moments again would happen where it was like, "Oh, yeah, my whiteness is also impacting this aspect" or "my experiences as a child really did create this formative thing in my head that whiteness isn't a race and that I'm just normal and average." And I had all these epiphany moments, these aha moments after writing because of the discussions we had.

Anna spoke of how the small group discussions allowed her to feel less alone in some of the negative feelings regarding racial issues that she revisited through writing about her memories. She said:

> Well, I think it helped me to understand that I wasn't alone . . . you know, there's a shame associated with things and decisions and thoughts you've had in my upbringing and past and racism around me. But that I'm not alone. A lot of us have experienced that. All of us has experienced it in some way, and that it's not about blame, it's about understanding where things come from . . . so that really helped me and it validated my feelings, you know, to be able to share it with people who were receptive in conversation and who

were willing to go beyond those lines again, like, you know. I think in the past some of the discussions I've had are very surface level and safe. And since the people that you know, you and Alex, when I was talking to you were willing to go past certain lines and past surface level, and talk really honestly, and it was, you know, an intimate small group.

She also spoke to how the small group discussions made her feel more accountable. She said:

This is the first time I did antiracist work in a small/intimate group and as a result-there was no way to hide from the work that needed to be done. I couldn't avoid the hard questions because there were only two of us answering them. I knew that discussion would follow within our group and that I would make up 1/3rd of that discussion. I think this was key in motivating me to examine my relationship to race so intimately and thoroughly rather than only on the surface like I had done in my past work.

8 Theoretical Implications and Implications for Teacher Development

This study explored the ways that writing personal narratives about their racial identity and engaging in small group discussions about this writing impacted the ability of two White educators to strengthen their racial competency. The participants began by writing about the implications of their race in their personal lives. They then transitioned to applying these experiences to their professional lives as educators. After considering these personal and professional implications, they then wrote about ways that they thought they could take these realizations and use them to create more authentically antiracist pedagogical practices. Lastly, the participants discussed the impact that writing had on their ability to increase their racial awareness and strengthen their racial competency. This chapter discusses implications for theory, implications for educator development, the limitations of the study, suggestions for future research, outlines goals for a potential professional practice product that stem from the results of this study, and the overall impact this study had on me as the researcher.

Theoretical Implications

The results of this study as they relate to theoretical implications correlate with the frameworks discussed in the literature review. Major theoretical concepts out of the field of CWS were discussed by my participants in their personal narratives, group discussions, and exit interviews. My participants also spoke to the power of racial self-inquiry as well as the transformative power of writing in general. The implications for these theoretical dispositions will be discussed further in this section.

CWS in Education

My participants spoke to many of the central concepts of CWS throughout the course of the study, namely the invisibility of whiteness, the normalization of whiteness, White supremacy, and White privilege. These concepts had implications for my participants in their personal and professional lives.

DOI: 10.4324/9781032659305-9

The Invisibility of Whiteness

As discussed in Chapter 2, the field of CWS focuses heavily on the invisible systems and structures that support White supremacy. Because whiteness is purposefully made to stay invisible in order to maintain a largely unquestioned dominance, it makes sense then that what it means to be White and the implications of whiteness often remain invisible to White people as individuals. Alex and Anna spoke to this notion throughout the course of the study. In nearly every piece of writing and group discussion, they spoke of having a complete lack of awareness regarding their racial identity and its impact on them and the world around them. In short, they spoke at length to the invisibility of whiteness; in being White and enjoying its privileges, what it actually meant to be White remained invisible to them.

I do want to challenge this idea of the invisibility of whiteness, however. While it is clear that Alex and Anna did not do much critical thinking about their whiteness throughout the course of their lives, I am not so sure that this means that whiteness and its implications were always invisible to them. It is clear through their discussion of moments from their past that Alex and Anna were able to identify and discuss at length instances where whiteness acted as a negative force in their lives and in the lives of people they interacted with. There is no doubt that the act of writing about these moments helped them to name issues of whiteness that they otherwise would not have analyzed. I will discuss this in more depth a bit later. However, I am also hard-pressed to believe that these issues were completely invisible to them when they occurred.

There is a difference between invisibility and willful ignorance. Alex and Anna even spoke about thinking about the negative implications of whiteness at the time that some of the events of their lives occurred. They just seemed to stop thinking at a certain point and moved on. In this way, issues of whiteness were not invisible to them. Like Baldwin said, White people have "set up in themselves a fantastic system of evasions, denials, and justifications, which system is about to destroy their grasp of reality, which is another way of saying their moral sense" ("The White Problem," 1964, as cited in Watson, 2013, p. 15). Evasions, denials, and justifications are deliberate actions; they are not passive brushes with an invisible whiteness. Alex and Anna discussed frequently the evasions, denials, and justifications they enacted in order to *keep* the implications of whiteness invisible to them. It turns out that the implications of whiteness were very much visible to Alex and Anna, and they worked rather hard to force them into invisibility. When seen in this way, the very active role that White people play in creating the illusion that whiteness is invisible makes the idea of the invisibility of whiteness all the more offensive to people of color, who see the very visible implications of whiteness in their lives on a daily basis through their lying outside the boundaries of whiteness.

The Normalization of Whiteness

Intimately connected to the notion of the invisibility of whiteness is the concept of the normalization of whiteness. As discussed in the literature review, the normalization of whiteness is the phenomenon where whiteness is used as the reference point for what is deemed "normal" in any particular context. Alex and Anna spoke to the normalization of whiteness in their personal lives, speaking again to their lack of awareness of their racial identity because they always saw being White as just "normal." However, as they became a bit more racially aware and entered the field of education, they saw how the schooling system also uses whiteness as the baseline for curriculum, assessments, pedagogy, and other educational activities. For example, Anna noticed that the dance curriculum privileged Western dance technique and that any suggestion by her to expand the curriculum to more diverse forms of dancing was quickly shot down. Her peers saw Western dance as the "normal" and "correct" way to teach students proper dance technique.

Keffrelyn D. Brown speaks to these issues in her book *After the At-Risk Label: Reorienting Educational Policy and Practice* (2016), where she demonstrates how the notion of educational "at-riskness" is a term often disproportionately reserved for students of color. Brown artfully shows how those students who fall outside the confines of educational normalcy (White, middle-class, etc.) are stigmatized as "other" and made inferior through an assumed level of ability based on comparing the student to the baseline of whiteness. Alex and Anna highlighted the normalization of whiteness in education along curricular, pedagogical, and disciplinary lines as they discussed their experiences in being educated and in being educators.

Perceived Level of Racial Competency

Alex and Anna were not at a ground-zero position when they entered this study. Both participants cited that they had thought about their racial identity and how it impacts their classrooms prior to being in the study. However, by the time the study ended, they were not as far along in their racial identity development as they had previously assumed. In other words, they found themselves to be much less racially competent than they initially believed. By the end of the study, they discussed how "they felt like they were doing the work," but it was not until writing their narratives and engaging in the group discussions that they realized how little work they had actually done.

Alex and Anna wore their level of racial competency as a badge of honor. Anna specifically saw herself as the most racially competent member of her department because of her experiences in other countries, learning about African dance, taking a class on James Baldwin, and dating a person of color. Alex also admitted that he saw himself as an ally in more performative ways, like listening to hip-hop music, having friends of color, and voting for Barack Obama. In this way, these personal experiences led Alex and Anna to feel like they were in a more racially aware position when they began teaching; they felt like they had less work to do than peers of theirs who did not have the experiences that they did. It was not until writing at length that they realized the surface-level nature of their racial awareness. I will discuss this idea of "liberal racially competent" teachers in more detail later in a later chapter.

White-on-White Abuse

Alex and Anna talked about abuse or the fear of suffering abuse at the hands of members of their White community, which deterred them from continuing to build their racial competency throughout the course of their lives. Thandeka (1999) discusses the abuse and fear of abandonment suffered by White children as they learn to be White. She posits that children learn to be White through the tutelage of their parents and other White community members. This learning ultimately comes with the threat of being abandoned by their White communities, which results in the child learning to maintain systems of whiteness for the sake of self-preservation. In short, Thandeka asserts that it is the desperate need to belong to their White communities that results in White people perpetuating White supremacy and White domination.

The threat of abandonment by their White communities and the impact this had on their ability to further develop their racial competency was discussed by Alex and Anna. While not explicitly stated, Alex talked about his wife's beliefs that were contrary to his at times regarding race and education. He said that his experience in the study made him see the importance of opening a dialogue with her rather than just letting their differences go for the sake of keeping the peace. Anna offered many instances of either being abused or fearing abandonment by her White family and teaching peers. She discussed how her parents did not support her relationship with a man of color when she was in college and how this impacted the relationship and her mental state. In her teaching career, she discussed many examples of her peers being explicitly racist. However, Anna rarely addressed these issues with her peers because she was afraid of how they would treat her as a result. Lastly, Anna talked about how her peers were consistently dismissive of her suggestions to teach non-Western dance forms. This resulted in her no longer trying to change the curriculum or doing smaller, less visible projects with smaller groups of students.

While not discussed explicitly by Alex and Anna, it is worth noting in this section that White-on-White abuse has become prevalent in the antiracist community in recent years. As a result of the presidency of Donald Trump, antiracist activists in a variety of fields have come to the forefront in much more public ways to create environments of racial justice. However, in taking on these antiracist causes and developing their antiracist identities, there are White antiracists who have made a habit of abusing other White antiracists for not being "antiracist enough." Professor Loretta J. Ross defines this phenomenon as "call out culture." She says:

> It's the tendency, which is unfortunate, for people to want to publicly shame and humiliate people. And it's based on what they say, or what they look like, or what they wear, or who they're hanging out with, or who they agree or disagree with. It's attaching labels to people without really doing any kind of nuance.
>
> (Scheimer & Chakrabarti, 2020)

She goes on to say that when people call out each other when they have the same goals as part of a movement, the movement becomes more like a cult. She says:

> [S]o when we indulge in the callout culture within our own movement, mainly because someone uses a word that we don't agree with, or they actually think that you should be focusing on the climate, while I'm focusing on reproductive justice, while I'm focused on racial justice, you're really trying to turn a movement—which is many different people thinking different thoughts and moving in the same direction—into a cult, which is many different people thinking the same thought and moving into a direction. And so we are a movement. We're not a cult. So I describe as a cult both places that don't allow dissent, that don't allow difference, that don't allow challenges, and don't even welcome critical skepticism.
>
> (Scheimer & Chakrabarti, 2020)

Tim Lensmire (2017) discusses this issue of antiracist call out culture as well. He writes:

> I worry that too much of the work of white anti-racists in teacher education and educational research doesn't actually escape this problem. Too often, instead of mobilizing other white people for anti-racist action, we use them, scapegoat them, to create our own anti-racist identities. I will let you sort out what proportion of anti-racist work done by white people with other white people is a scapegoating ritual; and what proportion of this scapegoating—ironically, tragically—is driven by fears of abandonment and desires for belonging.
>
> (p. 9)

Again, while these issues of White antiracist on White antiracist abuse were not explicitly cited by Alex and Anna, the issue was inadvertently touched on through their writing and discussions of other personal racial experiences. I will discuss this phenomenon in more detail in the final chapter of this book.

Racial Self-inquiry

The implications of engaging in racial self-inquiry to strengthen the racial competency of the White educators in my study were rather apparent. In line with Johnson's (2017) theory of racial storytelling, Alex and Anna's dive into their racial past allowed them to make clear connections between their racial identity and the decisions they made and will make in the classroom. The experiences of Alex and Anna in this study also spoke to Michael's (2015) ideas about the importance of asking difficult questions of the self over an extended period of time. While Alex and Anna engaged with these questions over a period of only four months, this was the longest duration of time that they ever engaged with queries of racial identity and participated in sustained conversations about racial identity. Alex and Anna both spoke to the impact of thinking about these issues in a consistent way over time. They said this created a practice for them that they hope will become a habit of reflecting daily about the ways in which their racial identity impacts their classrooms.

The Transformative Power of Writing

Writing a story from one's life forces the writer to organize the details of the narrative in a way that simply thinking about the story or retelling the story orally does not allow. When I think back to stories from my life, nothing in my brain is terribly linear. There are linear moments, but when it comes to thinking about a story or telling a story aloud, my brain quickly filters through a series of moments, that blip on the radar of my life, and the resulting story is what I made of those moments at that particular time. Chances are, because there would be no record of what I thought or said about the story, the next time I told it, it might look or sound quite different. Writing forces the writer to create a cohesive story that, at least for that particular piece of writing, remains unchanged.

The second feature of writing that lends itself to transformation for the writer is that there is a certain permanence to writing that is not present in thinking or speaking. I have had too many fleeting epiphanies in my life to count. I witness something, and I tell myself I will remember it because it has changed me; I will act differently and see the world more clearly from here on out because of this epiphany. But no sooner do I think about these things that I find myself making the same mistake or going back to my old ways. However, in the random moments that I have written about these epiphanies, forced myself to put on paper the degree to which I have been moved, had a change of heart, saw the world in a new way, there was a much better chance that I remained transformed. Where thinking or speaking about a moment that changed me often results in a temporary transformation, writing about a moment that changed me (even less formally as in journal form) resulted in a more permanent transformation. If I ever forgot about what this moment did for my outlook on living, all I needed to do was look back at my writing. Writing grounds the plot points of one's transformation. It makes them more real and unable to be ignored.

Lastly, the act of writing forces the writer to sit with their thoughts much longer and consider them more critically than the act of thinking or speaking. Having to work through how one wants to convey a story in writing is a laborious task, one that inevitably results in having to sit with one's thoughts a lot longer than most people want to. I am ashamed at the number of times that I have shot off at the mouth with an ill-pondered thought, the implications of which I had no idea. As I look back on my life, I often wonder about things I may have never said (or may have said in a different way) had I written them down first. Conversely, I often think about writing things I would never say aloud and have no interest in thinking about how they impact my life and the lives of people around me. While writing these things out might be a painful and scary process, it is in the physical act of writing a part of a story, erasing that part of the story, rewriting that part of the story, having to sit longer with that part of the story, and ultimately committing to the page that part of the story that a more fully realized mirror to the self is created.

Writing was the main tool utilized by Alex and Anna to engage in racial self-inquiry. In this way, there were also theoretical implications with regard to the act of writing as a means to strengthen the racial competency of White teachers. The following sections detail how the act of writing impacted Alex and Anna's ability to process their racial realities in relation to the features of transformative writing described above.

Increased Awareness and Understanding: Writing as a Way of Seeing

Writing in a critical and in-depth fashion about their racial identity allowed Alex and Anna to see the impact of their racial identity in their personal and professional lives in ways they had not seen before. In line with Harris (2004), Alex and Anna came to a deeper understanding of the impact that their race has on their personal and professional worlds through the written word. The results of this study are also supported by the work of Raab (2014). Raab discussed how writing memoirs about their experiences resulted in bringing a deeper meaning to the lives of her participants. Alex and Anna spoke to this idea throughout the course of the study. They asserted that they would never have made the connections about their lives that they did if they had just thought about their experiences instead of writing about them. Their writing was a site to better organize experiences from their lives, which allowed them to make connections between experiences they had not made before. These connections unveiled to them deeper meanings for their lives as their racial experiences came to present themselves as much more nuanced than they had originally thought prior to putting pen to paper. I call this increased awareness and depth of understanding about the implications of their racial identity as an enhanced way of seeing their worlds and how they interact with them as White people.

Increased Motivation to Act: Writing as a Way of Being

Where increased awareness and understanding correlates to a way of seeing, acting on this newfound awareness and understanding results in a new way of being. The increased motivation to act on their discoveries of self was a result of Alex and Anna's writing process. Yagelski (2009) notes the potential for writing to be an agent of individual and collective change for the writer if done authentically and honestly. Both Alex and Anna spoke with excitement for what comes next once the study ended. They wanted to take what they learned about themselves personally and professionally regarding their racial identities and apply this new knowledge to their lives in order to create change in their lives and in the lives of the people around them, namely their students. Good teachers are change agents. They come into the profession believing they can change the students in their classrooms and thus change the world. Alex and Anna are good teachers who wholeheartedly believe this as well. However, they came to realize through their writing that one cannot change the world if they do not do the hard work of changing themselves. The disciplined practice of constant self-reflection is required in order to consider the ways in which one needs to change as an individual so that they can change the world. Personal narrative writing allows the writer to come to better ontological cognizance. This personal writing gives the writer the ability to see who they are, why they are, what they want out of life, and what one might need to change in order to attain this. It is only possible to change the world if one changes oneself as an individual first. Alex and Anna came to realize this, and it was the act of writing that allowed them to think more deeply about ontological shifts that could lead to change outside of themselves.

Implications for Teacher Development

The results of this study also spoke to implications for teacher development. Alex and Anna made many comparisons to their experiences in the study to prior teacher development training. This section further details how Alex and Anna's experiences in the study enhanced their understanding of their racial identity in ways that prior professional development opportunities did not.

The Time to Write: The Use of Prolonged Reflective Writing

In many professional development trainings for teachers, there is little time to reflect in meaningful ways. Because these training sessions are often expensive, school administrators try to get as much "accomplished" as possible in these training sessions. Many times, the result of this is a surface-level training marked by surface-level teacher reflection at best. Not to mention that the teachers sitting in these trainings are in the midst of a school year where they are most likely behind on lesson planning, grading, and other areas of teacher preparation. This combination of rushed training and a group of teachers whose minds are elsewhere makes for an experience that lacks depth and does not promote authentic change.

Alex and Anna wrote and spoke about how beneficial it was to them to have the time to engage in the writing process in a thorough way. Because we began the study at the end of the school year and carried it through the summer, Alex and Anna felt much more capable of dedicating meaningful time to their writing and our conversations. They did not feel rushed or overwhelmed because they had a month to write each section of their narrative without having to focus on their teaching at the same time. The results of this study were clear: engaging in prolonged writing and discussion sessions over the summer benefited Alex and Anna in ways that professional development during the school year did not. I argue that giving teachers the opportunity to do training on racial identity over the summer will result in a more meaningful experience for the teachers. Many teachers are required to attain a certain number of professional development hours per year. If teachers could apply these summer hours to the school year, they not only would have an incentive to use the flex professional development time that they attained over the summer to prep, plan, or grade during the school year, but the result of doing the training over the summer might result in a more authentic learning experience as well.

A Space to Share: The Use of Small Group Discussions

Not only is there little time afforded to teachers in many professional development training sessions, but there is also little opportunity to engage in meaningful small group discussions. Yes, breakout sessions are a common trait of professional development training. But these sessions run for 15 minutes at the most before teachers head back to the larger group. Teachers are also often paired with faculty and staff members that they do not know well enough to be vulnerable. Teachers may even be asked to engage in different small groups throughout the duration of the session, so there is no way to build even a little trust with the same group of people throughout the course of the training. These characteristics all come together to create small group settings that lack authentic and meaningful conversations.

Alex and Anna discussed in great detail the benefits of our small group discussions. They both liked that we had an hour or so slated for each meeting. Because our group was only three people, this allowed everyone's voice to be heard and responded to in authentic ways. They both said that the small group also created a sense of accountability that having this experience in a larger group would not have created. They knew that they were going to make up a third of the conversation and that they were going to be expected to speak to the writing that they did over the course of the month. Lastly, they felt that the environment we created as a group allowed them to be vulnerable and honest, which helped lead them to a greater potential for personal change. This trust was not built in one session, however. This trust was built over time as we met more and more. This sustained time to meet with the same group of people is not typically a part of professional development training, but it was something that both Alex and Anna came to appreciate and cited as being integral to their development throughout the duration of the study.

Scaffolded Race Inquiry Groups

Teachers come to professional development training with a certain set of experiences and awareness regarding the topics being covered in the training. For example, some teachers may have already had the introductory training on the slate for that particular professional development day. This results in a waste of time for the teacher and a tough day for the presenter if the majority of the faculty and staff had done their training previously. This notion is no different for equity, diversity, inclusion, and racial identity development training.

In order for any training to be meaningful for the participants, the administration who books the training and the presenter must know their audience. The presenter needs to know what their audience already knows in order to respect the time of the teachers and create the most meaningful experience. Alex and Anna spoke to how they felt we were not doing any surface-level work from the start, something they felt they did time and time again in prior professional development training. This was because I knew my audience. I knew the training Alex and Anna had done in the past and had a general feel for the knowledge they were bringing to the study. The results of this study showed the benefits of scaffolding professional development training depending on what the teachers already know coming into the training. For example, if a staff of 200 teachers is about to participate in an introductory equity training, it might be worth figuring out who did similar training in the past and creating groups of teachers to do different activities based on their prior professional development experiences. We differentiate instruction for students, but we rarely do this for teachers in professional development training.

Potential Professional Development Model: Integration of Critical Reflection on White Racial Identity and Implementation of District-wide White Racial Inquiry Groups

White teachers must strengthen their racial competency through deep self-reflection in order to navigate issues of equity, diversity, inclusion, and race in their classrooms. This reflection of the racial self allows White teachers to see the ways they are personally impacted by their whiteness and, thus, how their whiteness affects all aspects of their classroom. This was clear in the experiences of Alex and Anna. The following is a sample action plan for any district interested in incorporating this critical reflection of White teachers into the current equity, diversity, and inclusion (EDI) professional development plan of the district. The plan also offers a model for establishing White affinity groups across the district where White teachers can reflect on their racial development journey.

Mission

To make Whiteness and its impacts on education visible through deep reflections of the self and teacher pedagogies to foster an equitable and inclusive learning community.

Vision

1. Reflect deeply about the impact of race in the personal lives of White teachers.
2. Reflect deeply about how the way race plays a part in the personal lives of teachers affects what and how they teach.
3. Off these reflections, have White teachers identify and implement antiracist strategies in the classroom and in the school.

Values

1. Uncover the invisibility of whiteness and systemic oppression in education by making conversations about race in the school the norm, not the exception.
2. Challenge the denial of White complicity in education by ushering White teachers to engage in personal and professional reflections about how they may unwittingly contribute to upholding these systems of oppression in their classrooms.
3. As a school, move beyond pedagogies of White privilege and develop more multifaceted antiracist pedagogies by asking teachers to be critical of the systems that allow for White privilege in the first place.

Goals

1. Assess current EDI professional development trainings and look for gaps in White teacher identity work.
2. Develop reflective activities that ask White teachers to consider the impact their race has on their personal lives and the lives of their students.

3. Implement these activities throughout the course of the year as part of the greater EDI professional development trainings.
4. Develop smaller White racial inquiry groups across the district that meet consistently and align with the mission, vision, and goals of the action plan.
5. Collect data from the EDI professional development training and race inquiry groups in order to measure the impact of the critical self-reflection on the lives of the White teachers and their classrooms.

Action Steps and Time Frame

This sample plan assumes that the district already has in place an EDI office or committee. If this is not yet an integral part of the district leadership, this group should be established first.

June

Hold a meeting of the district EDI committee where committee members brainstorm ways to add discussions/activities to EDI professional development that focus on strengthening the racial competency of White teachers. Members should take note of the importance of providing sufficient *time* for this authentic critical self-inquiry of White teachers. The committee should identify facilitators for professional development, which include both White people and people of color. It should also develop a survey in conjunction with professional development activities to be distributed after professional development sessions. A draft of this plan should be due at the end of July.

July

The district EDI committee reviews the draft of the EDI professional development plan. Further suggestions/alterations are discussed at this meeting. The final plan is adopted at the end of the month by the school board.

August

The first activities on White teacher identity occur during "Back to School Week" for teachers. Distribute the survey at the end of the session.

September

The district EDI committee reviews survey results from the initial White teacher identity session. The committee will use this data to better inform how to go about structuring the race inquiry groups for White teachers.

October

The district EDI committee begins the development of district-wide race inquiry groups for White teachers. The committee will create a call for volunteers and identify faculty and staff who would be interested in helping to create the groups and/or being a part of the groups.

November

The district EDI committee meets with the race inquiry committee to develop a timeline for meetings and meeting activities. Both the EDI committee and the race inquiry group committee should work together to develop a survey that district staff will complete after the inquiry group sessions are completed.

December

The district EDI committee and race inquiry committee meet to adopt the race inquiry group model. The schedule for meetings is sent out to participants prior to winter break.

January–April

The first race inquiry group is held across the district. Meetings occur once per month until the end of the year. Summer meetings are offered but not required. Consider any summer meetings counting toward continued education hours or flex professional development hours.

May

The survey is distributed to the ace inquiry group members across the district. The survey is due the first week of June.

June

The district EDI committee and race inquiry group committee meet to review and assess survey results. The results are used to gauge the impact that participating in the race inquiry groups had on the White teachers personally and pedagogically.

Reference List

Baldwin, J. (2010). The white problem. In R. Kenan (Ed.), *The cross of redemption* (pp. 72–79). Pantheon Books. (Original work published 1964).

Brown, K. D. (2016). *After the "at-risk" label: Reorienting educational policy and practice*. Teachers College Press.

Harris, R. (2004). Encouraging emergent moments: The personal, critical, and rhetorical in the writing classroom. *Pedagogy: Critical Approaches to Teaching Literature, Language Composition, and Culture, 4*(3), 401–418.

Johnson, L. L. (2017). The racial Hauntings of one black male professor and the disturbance of the self(ves): Self-Actualization and racial storytelling as pedagogical practices. *Journal of Literacy Research, 49*(4), 476–502. https://doi.org/10.1177/1086296x17733779

Lensmire, T. J. (2017). White anti-racists and belonging. *Whiteness and Education, 2*(1), 4–14. http://dx.doi.org/10.1080/23793406.2017.1361304

Michael, A. (2015). *Raising race questions: Whiteness and inquiry in education*. Teachers College Press.

Raab, D. (2014). Creative transcendence: Memoir writing for transformation and empowerment. *The Journal of Transpersonal Psychology, 46*(2), 1–21.

Scheimer, D., & Chakrabarti, M. (2020, December 3). *Why scholar Loretta Ross is 'calling in' callout culture*. www.wbur.org/onpoint/2020/12/03/feminist-scholar-loretta-ross-is-calling-out-cancel-culture

Thandeka. (1999). *Learning to be white: Money, race, and god in America*. Bloomsbury.

Watson, V. T. (2013). *The souls of white folk: African American writers theorize whiteness*. University Press of Mississippi.

Yagelski, R. P. (2009). A thousand writers writing: Seeking change through the radical practice of writing as a way of being. *English Education, 42*(1), 6–28.

9 A Lifetime of Critically Reflective Work
Swimming Upstream

No Finish Line in Sight

There are two characteristics of racial identity development work that make it personally and professionally challenging for White people. First, there is no finish line; there is only progress that is the result of sustained personal reflection and intimate (often uncomfortable) conversations with others, particularly with people of color. Thinking about the impact of one's racial identity does not necessarily come naturally to White folks. When a White person does begin to come to terms with the fact that they do indeed have a racial identity and that it has serious implications, it can often become the case that a well-intentioned White person begins to look for a checklist of things to read, videos to watch, and tasks to accomplish that would tell them they have arrived at their full-realized racialized self. I have found this to be particularly true for educators when it comes to many educational "initiatives." Teachers tend to come into professional development disgruntled about the content to begin with and want a flowchart that "just tells them what to do" so that they can say they did what is required of them. It all feels like "just another thing" teachers are being asked to do on top of all the other things they do on a daily basis. I suppose if there is any goal of racial development work, it is not that there is any specific end to it but rather that it does not come to feel like "doing another thing" at all; it becomes a way of being.

When I tell White folks that racial development work never ends, I am sometimes met with much resistance to the idea. I understand how this can feel like some sort of trap for a White person, especially in the polarized world we live in today. If there is no "certificate" of racial competency, then there is always the possibility of making a mistake, always the possibility of getting it wrong, and always the possibility of doing harm. It can feel incredibly difficult to commit to something for a lifetime and to constantly personally reflect in deep and authentic ways, knowing that there is still more to learn and more ways to be better. The fact is that this is the nature of racial development work. Actually, the fact is that this is the nature of any part of our identity that is a part of our way of being. Ways of being have no finish line; ways of being require always being open to learning opportunities, consistent and authentic reflection, and waking up each day striving to be a bit better than yesterday. Ways of being come with triumphs and mistakes. And as I tell my students, there is nothing wrong with making a mistake; there is something very wrong about not learning from it, however.

Don't get me wrong. I typically like finish lines. They give me a tangible goal I can see even if it is far in the distance. Crossing the finish line gives me a clear sense of accomplishment and purpose. But how often do the things we define ourselves most strongly by, our ways of being, come with finish lines? How often do they come with utter clarity? How often do they come with the feelings of "I am done, I have arrived, and I have come to know all that is possible about this part of myself"? There are many days I wish I had a checklist for what it means to be a fully realized father, teacher, or husband. But what ultimately makes me better in these ways of being I hold so dear is something that could never be written in a checklist. It is in the journey. It is in the excitement of knowing when you did good work. It is also in the terror of the next day when you know you made a mistake. And it is in the triumph of reflecting on this mistake and knowing that given the same opportunity again, you will be better next time.

Socrates famously said, "the unexamined life is not worth living." Being a more racially competent person only comes from committing to a lifelong examination and reexamination of the self. If we are willing to do this in order to be more successful in our ways of being as parents, teachers, partners, friends, and family members, then we might have more of the skills necessary than we think to build our racial competency. But like all parts of ourselves we see worth developing over a lifetime, we need to first see our racial identity as something important enough to develop over a lifetime. I hope that by reading about Alex and Anna's experiences of reflecting on their racial identity you have been able to see the value of this work as educators and as people. It is our responsibility as educators to reflect on who and why we are throughout the course of our careers to ensure that we continue to grow and continue to be as effective as possible in the classroom. While our racial identity is only one part of who we are, it is big enough, complex enough, and important enough to develop as part of becoming the best educators we can be. This is especially true for White educators, who may have spent the majority of their lives never once considering their racial identity while being in front of students of color who have thought about their racial identity every day of their conscious lives for a variety of reasons.

Too Much or Not Enough: The Politics of Racial Identity Work

The second characteristic that makes racial identity development work challenging for White people is the highly political and polarizing nature of the work outside and inside schools. It goes without saying that having district- and building-level administrators who are supportive of racial identity development and antiracist practices makes bringing them into the classroom much easier. But even in the most supportive of districts and buildings, this work is challenged by students, parents, and colleagues who tell them it is something not worth teachers thinking about and certainly has no place in the classroom. We live in a world where the introduction of the College Board's new AP African American Studies curriculum came under scrutiny for purging the names of many Black writers and scholars associated with CRT and some politically fraught topics, like Black Lives Matter. This comes on the heels of states across the country calling for books to be banned that highlight the voices of marginalized people.

At the time I write this, among the 26 states that have banned books, my home state of Pennsylvania ranks second in the country in book-ban incidents. At the same time, the PA State Board of Education has approved nine culturally relevant and sustaining competencies that teachers will be required to demonstrate in their classrooms. This speaks to the complex and polarized nature of racial identity work in my state and beyond, as groups who advocate against inclusive texts, antiracist pedagogies, and racial identity development work attend board meetings to speak out while proponents of inclusive texts work to ensure that creating culturally sustaining spaces and curricula is a legal standard in some states.

However, White people are challenged from the other end too, as they are sometimes told (even when they are authentically trying) that they are getting it wrong and that they are not doing enough to develop their racial identity. Both well-intentioned and disingenuous White antiracists have the capacity to call out other White people who are not developing on their timeline. As I said in the introduction to this book, there is a difference between a White person who is called out for overt racist behavior or ignoring repeated requests to reconsider their attitudes and a White person who is authentically attempting to develop their racial identity but makes an honest mistake. The fact that we sometimes have trouble discerning the difference comes at the expense of potentially stopping someone's racial development journey dead in its tracks.

The scrutiny that comes with "doing too much or not enough" as it relates to racial development work as a White educator makes it challenging to want to continue the work at all. It can very much feel like one is continually swimming upstream and fighting a losing battle. To use the analogy of parenthood again, I can always find a social media thread after making a parental choice that can either vilify or applaud me for said choice. "How dare you allow your toddler time on an electronic device," one group might say, while the other says, "Good on the parent who responsibly prepares their child for the technological world they have entered into by allowing them time with electronic devices." The following points have helped me when my racial development work has been challenged by others one way or the other:

1. First, I reflect again on my purpose. Have I been authentic in the work, or is there something else that might be inauthentic (even subconsciously) at the heart of why I am doing what I am doing?

2. If my purpose is authentically aligned, I then reflect on the criticism. I also consider the source of the criticism. If I made a mistake, the person criticizing me has a valid point, and the purpose of their criticism is to support me. I look at this as an opportunity to further develop my racial competency.
3. If the criticism comes from someone who sees no value at all in racial development work or someone who is just trying to have a contest about who is more antiracist, then I cannot spend much time on it. The value of this work is not in convincing someone who could care less that their racial identity is worth exploring or in convincing someone that I am more racially aware than them. This leads me to a final point. . .
4. I always try to remember that the value of this work is in spending my time continuing to develop my racial competency in order to support my growth as a person and an educator. The paradox here is that in deeply reflecting on the personal impact of my racial identity, I am actually able to better serve those around me. Inward reflection creates outward transformation. This is the ultimate goal of racial development work for me: to better know myself so that I can better understand and support the people around me.

Some Words of Reality and Some Words of Encouragement

I need to be clear in these final words: the work of developing one's racial competency feels like an impossible task at times. As you explore your racial self, especially through the intimate act of writing, there will be many personal challenges that arise. There will be feelings of guilt and shame that come with recounting the stories of your racial past as a White person, moments of wishing you had done one thing or the other instead of something that proved to be harmful. There will be feelings of anger toward yourself when recounting moments that you feel you should have done more to support those in positions of less power. There will be feelings of confusion in the face of things you might not yet understand. There might be even frustration when you find out that as a White person, you will *never* be able to understand some things in full.

There will be many interpersonal challenges on your journey to better develop your racial competency as well. Naysayers will say that the hard work you are doing to develop your racial competency is no more than leftist propaganda aimed at making White people feel bad about being White. You will be told by these same people that exploring racial identity should be no part of a teacher's practice. In some cases, you might even be told that any mention of identity at all does not belong in schools and that any instance of "identity politics" in the classroom is an instance of indoctrination that only makes us more "divisive." And supposed proponents of this work might tell you that you are doing it "incorrectly" or that you are not taking it "seriously" enough, even when you know you are truly trying. You might be told you aren't "radical" enough in your exploration of the self and subsequent pedagogical choices. There could be times where you are told you are just being "performative" in your work; you might not even know what this means or what it looks like.

With potential doubts coming from yourself, from people who do not believe in your work, and from people who *say* they support your work, it might very well be the case that you get to a point where you see the work as pointless and want to quit. If you get to this point, I want you to think about one word: purpose. *Why* is it that you are going on this racial development journey in the first place? In here lies another way that writing is a phenomenal tool for those of us who believe in the true power of developing racial competency. While critically important, the page is not just a place where you can look back and connect the dots of your racial identity all the way to your present. It is also a place where you can better define your future as a more racially competent person by asserting and reasserting your purpose in doing the work whenever you feel like you have lost sight of your goals.

In her book *Textured Teaching: A Framework for Culturally Sustaining Practices*, Lorena Escoto Germán asks readers:

> What does it mean to welcome the whole of humanity of our students into our classrooms? How can we create spaces where they are authentically themselves? What does it look like to shift away from upholding standards created by someone else that only serve to minimize our students? To do this, we need to honor the wholeness of people. We have to see and respect all the elements of who we are.
>
> (p. 129)

When you do reflect on the purpose of your racial identity development work in your times of doubt, I hope that you ultimately come to this fact: doing this work is about honoring and respecting everything about who your *students* are. You cannot do this for your students, however, until you commit to reflecting for a lifetime on all the elements of who *you* are, an important one of which is your racial identity. So in those moments of personal struggle and interpersonal challenges, I urge you to remember that in the constant work of becoming a more fully realized educator and person by developing your racial competency, you are also doing the transformative work of guiding your students to find their more fully realized selves. I hope that reading this book has allowed you to begin to see how the act of writing offers unique and powerful opportunities to do this.

Reference List

Germán, L. E. (2021). *Textured teaching: A framework for culturally sustaining practices*. Heinemann.

Index

abandonment, fear 59–60
accountability: sense, creation 64–65; tool, writing (usage) 53
action research: broad view 32; narrative inquiry, interconnectedness 32
action steps (time frame) 67–68
After the At-Risk Label (Brown) 58
American culture, Whiteness (meaning) 5–6
Angelou, Maya 2
antiracism/antiracist: activity 47; classrooms, creation 47; identities, creation 60; practice 26, 46; strategies, implementation 66; teachers 46, 48, 54; term (usage) 12; undermining 24; work (small/intimate group) 55
antiracist education: Critical Whiteness Studies (CWS), relationship 22–24; definition 23; setting/spaces 23, 41; theoretical underpinning 16
AP African American Studies curriculum (College Board introduction) 72
awareness: absence 37–38; increase 50–51, 62–63

Baldwin, James 2, 18–19, 57–58
being, writing (impact) 50, 63
Black, being (jokes) 39
Black gaze, control (right) 20
Black Lives Matter 2, 3; supporters, White nationalist threats 20–21
Black man, storytelling 25
Black people, invisibility 20
Black Skin, White Masks (Fanon) 19
Brown, Keffrelyn D. 58

call out culture (call-out culture) 60; instances 6
cancel culture, instances 6
Chestnutt, Charles 18
Clandinin, Jean 28
classroom: antiracist classrooms, creation 47; antiracist strategies, implementation 66; education, Whiteness presence (combatting) 47; instruction, impact 46; race discussion, study opportunity 48–49; students, welcoming (meaning) 74; Whiteness honesty 48, 53–54
Color, privilege (absence) 17
community, creation 47–48
Critical Race Theory (CRT) 3, 11, 16–17; discussion 16; impact 14, 17; literature, review 16
Critical Whiteness Studies (CWS) 3, 11, 17–19; antiracist education, relationship 22–24; CRT assumptions, usage 18; definition 17; discussion 16; focus, aim 18; impact 14; literature, review 16; research, grounding 13; second wave, impact 9–10; teacher identity, relationship 24; theoretical framework 13; usage 56
cross-racial relationships: engagement 12; issues, handling 6–7; reciprocity 12; skills/confidence 26

dance, discipline (impact) 48–49
data collection: methods, multiplicity 33; procedures 33–34
denials, system 19, 57

Index

DiAngelo, Robin 19, 23
district-wide white racial inquiry groups, implementation 65–66
diversity: issues, navigation 65–66; work 43
Dubois, W.E.B. 18–19

education: antiracist educational spaces (creation), Whiteness barrier (impact) 41; Critical Whiteness Studies (CWS), usage 56; initiatives 70; normalcy 58; passivity 43; White anti-racists, work (impact) 60; Whiteness 9–10; Whiteness (combatting) 46, 47; Whiteness, connection 41–42; White system, interaction 10
education system: domination, Whiteness (impact) 34; historical construction/limitations, awareness 48; shortcomings 48
epiphanies 52–53, 61; concreteness 52; moments 54; realization, writing (impact) 35
equity, diversity, and inclusion (EDI) committee: district-wide race inquiry groups, development 68; draft review 67; race inquiry group committee, interaction 68
equity, diversity, and inclusion (EDI) professional development: plan 66; trainings 66–67
equity, issues (navigation) 65–66
Escoto Germán, Lorena 74
evasions, system 19, 57
experiences: application 56; depth 51; personal level, racial identity (impact) 34; stories 28

Fanon, Frantz 19
feedback: openness 26; request 12
feelings: discussion 2–3; inadequacy 43; validation 54–55
Floyd, George (murder) 1, 3
Frankenburg, Ruth 18, 20

Giovanni, Nikki 2
group meetings: characteristics 35; participation 11

hegemonic racial structure 9–10
history: minority groups, racialization 17; teaching 2; white history, teaching 42; whiteness/racial identity, discussion 20; White supremacy, creation 21
holistic antiracist pedagogies: development 11; usage 34
hooks, bell 20
Hurston, Zora Neale 18

identities: multiplicity, tenet 17; work, gaps (search) 66
identity politics 73–74
"I'm not a racist" surface mindset 51
inclusion, issues (navigation) 64–65

jokes, making 38–39
justifications, system 19, 57

Kendi, Ibram X. 22
knowledge: providing 48; value 54
Ku Klux Klan members, marches 20

Lensmire, Tim 60
Leonardo, Zeus 22
literal existence 52
living/telling 32; acts 13

McIntosh, Peggy 18, 21, 47
Michael, Ali 25, 26
Mills, Charles W. 21
minority: shape/form 40; status, tenet 17
minority groups: domination 23; racialization, tenet 17
Morrison, Toni 18, 19
motivation: absence 43; increase 63
movement, cult characteristic 60

narrative inquiry: action research, interconnectedness 31–32; connections 32; definition 28; methodology 16; process, description 28; researcher approach 28; tradition, research design (relationship) 31

Obama, Barack (vote) 39
oppression: form 12; jokes, usage 38
"Other" 20

participants, description 32–33
people: perspectives, hearing (value) 54; superiority, assumption 12; wholeness, honoring 74
personal lives, change (creation) 31–32
personal narratives 34–35; discussion 11; tool 26–27
personal narratives, writing 11–13, 26, 63; impact 41
personal/professional life, race issues (addressing) 54
person of color (people of color): advantages, absence 12; culture 39; dating 58–59; offensiveness 57; un-whiteness 20
positive racism 38
positive white racial identity 12
power: race/racism relationship, study/transformation 11; realization 51
privilege: enjoyment, reminder 40; fearlessness, privilege 41; white privilege 12, 21, 23
privileged life, existence 8–9
professional development: goals 66–67; mission 66; model 65–66; values 66; vision 66
professional development training 64–65; ineffectiveness 44–45; scaffolding, benefit 65
prolonged reflective writing, usage 63–65
public racial life, private racial life (contrast) 38–39
purpose: authentic alignment 73; reflection 72

Raab, Diana 27
race: awareness 33, 40, 56; beliefs 39; discussion, opportunities (increase) 48; discussion, student opportunity 48–49; dynamics, noticing/analyzing 12, 26; feelings 51; focus 4; inquiry groups 35, 65; issues 37–38, 53, 54, 64–65; personal narratives, writing 11; personal/professional relationship, understanding 51; question, scarcity 37; racism/power, relationships (study/transformation) 11; reflection, depth 66; relationship 51; social thought/relation product 17; thoughts 51; understanding 52; Whiteness, contrast 54; white teacher consideration 66
Race, Whiteness, and Education (Leonardo) 22
racial competence 12; definition 26; development 43; ability 37–38; improvement, journey 73–74; journey 5–7; level 58–59; strengthening 39, 50, 56, 62; teacher ability 46; whiteness barrier, impact 37, 41
Racial Contract, The (Mills) 21
racial development work: challenges 72–73; continuation 70
racial identity: articulation 23; awareness 37–38, 50–51; critical self-reflection, district-wide implementation (action plan) 7; development 58, 70, 71–72; discussion 20; impact 5, 34–36; internal conflict 10; processing 40; processing ability 39; queries, engagement 61; reflecting, benefit 47; reflecting, writing/discussion (impact) 34–35; understanding, depth 51; unseen implications 1; work, politics 71–73
racial inequality, relations (interruption) 10–11
racial issues: addressing, passivity 43; negative feelings 54–55
racialization: constitution, White interdependence 22–23; making 39–40
racially reflective journey: data analysis procedures 36; data collection procedures 33–34; exit interviews 35; participants, description 32–33; personal narratives 34–35; researcher role 36; setting 32; study 31
racial self-inquiry 12, 61
racial stereotypes: danger 39–40; escape 40
racial storytelling 13; act 16; model 25
racism: actions 43–44; definition 12; harm 54; historical construct, education (relationship) 42;

issue, awareness 51; location 23; oppression 12; positive racism 38; problem, size/complexity 43–44; race/power relationship, study/transformation 11; tenet 17
racist jokes, telling: sentiments 39; shame 38
reality: composing/recomposing, language (usage) 26; creation, writing (impact) 52
reflective activities: development 66; implementation 67
relationships, building 47–48
"Representing Whiteness in the Black Imagination" (hooks) 20
reproductive justice, focus 60
researcher: positionality 8–9; role 36
retelling/reliving 32; acts 13
Roediger, David 18
Ross, Loretta J. 60

safe zone, life 52
scapegoating ritual 60
school: antiracist strategies, implementation 66; secondary 42; training 45; Whiteness 40
second-wave White teacher identity studies 24
seeing, writing (impact) 50, 62–63
self: composing, language (usage) 26; conception 10
self-doubt 74
self-inquiry: depth 28; process 16, 25
shame: presence 54–55; public shame/humiliation 60
skin color, worldview contextualization 9
small-group discussions: beauty 54; benefits 54–55; importance 47; usage 64–65
small/intimate group (antiracist work) 55
social critique 26
social interaction 28
social repercussions, fear 44–45
sociopolitical context: book, situating 3–5; study, situating 13–14
Socrates 71
Souls of White Folk, The (Watson) 18
space, sharing 64–65
stereotypes. *see* racial stereotypes
story(telling): example 1; living/telling 16, 32; racial 13; retelling/reliving 32; telling, request 13; version, belief 19

students: conversations/expression 48–49; essay, critical pedagogy 26; humanity, welcoming (meaning) 74; minimization 74; race discussion opportunity 48–49
students of color 41; family life, contrast 5–6

teachers: antiracist teacher, meaning 46; education, white anti-racist work (impact) 60; identity, Critical Whiteness Studies (relationship) 24; personal lives, race (impact) 66; professional level (experiences), racial identity (impact) 34; self-knowledge, importance 25; White teachers, racial self-inquiry (approach) 25–26
teachers, development: impact 46; implications 56, 63; theoretical implications 56
teaching: capacities, multiplicity 33; tweak 51
terminology 11–12
Textured Teaching (Escoto Germán) 74
theoretical framework 13
theoretical underpinnings 16
thoughts: differences 60; organizational tool, writing (usage) 53
tools, providing 48
training: meaningfulness 65; personal development training 64; sessions, expense 63–64
transformation 61–62; initiation 10
trope, emergence 18
Trump, Donald (antiracist activist presence, increase) 59–60

understanding: depth 51; increase 62–63
unexamined life (Socrates) 71
upbringing, impact 39–40
U.S. Capital, White terrorists (attack) 21

Watson, Veronica T. 18
Weisel, Elie 2
White-led CWS movement, impact 18
White nationalists, threats 20–21
Whiteness: addressing, passivity 43; averageness, false belief 42; barrier 37, 41; baseline, establishment 42; combatting,

teacher development/classroom instruction (impact) 46; consideration 10; culture, discussion 20; discouragement, feeling 43–44; educational standard, positioning 42; education, connection 41–42; effects, invisibility 32; hegemonic racial structure 9–10; honesty 48, 53–54; impacts, analysis 25; invisibility 56, 57; invisibility, uncovering 66; material/psychological advantages 12, 19; normalization 20–22, 56, 58; norms, valuation 42; presence, combatting 47; problem, size/complexity 43–44; protection 40; race, contrast 54; reckoning, absence 42; relationship 51; school usage 58; standard, dictation 42; studying, goals 23; term, defining 11–12; theoretical underpinning 16; understanding 52; visibility 18; white racial identity, relationship 19–20; white teacher processing 11; worries, absence 27–28

White-on-White abuse 4, 59–60

White people: advantages 12; anti-racists 4–5, 60; communities 4, 40; complicity, denial (challenge) 66; domination, system 3–4, 14, 21, 34; identity 9–10, 18; interdependence 22–23; power 37; power, invisibility 4; race, haunting 25; racial inquiry groups, development 67; racial self-inquiry, personal narrative (tool) 26–27; safety, imagining 20; schooling 37; student, experiences 41–42; suburbia, existence 40; superiority, creation/reinforcement 19; terrorists, Capitol attack 21; unintentional harm 6

White privilege 12, 23, 56; confessions 9; discourses 22; impact 41; invisible weightless knapsack, comparison 21; meaning, CWS examination 11; normalization 20–22; pedagogies 11, 22, 66

White racial identity: critical reflection, integration 65–66; layers 19; model 25–26; Whiteness, relationship 19–20

White supremacy 12, 56; creation, domination system (impact) 21; ideology, entrenchment 20; invisible structure 3; normalization 20–22; term, discussion 20

White teachers: antiracist strategies, implementation 66; district-wide race inquiry groups, development 68; identity studies 24; identity work, gaps (search) 66; personal lives, race (impact) 66; positive racial identity, development 25; race, impact (consideration) 66; racial identity, researcher approach 28; racial self-inquiry, approach 25–26

whitewashing 37

willful ignorance, invisibility (contrast) 57

writing: act/action 27, 52–53, 62; being function 50, 63; empowerment/motivation 53–54; experience 35; feeling 52; impact 27, 47, 52; permanence 61–62; point writing, elaboration 42; project, significance 10–11; racial identity, reflecting 34–35; seeing function 50, 62–63; spark 51; time, determination/duration 63–65; transformative power 7, 10, 16, 26–27, 61–62; usage 53; vehicle 10; way of being 10–11

writing process 51, 52, 63; empowerment 53; engagement 64

For Product Safety Concerns and Information please contact our EU representative GPSR@taylorandfrancis.com
Taylor & Francis Verlag GmbH, Kaufingerstraße 24, 80331 München, Germany

www.ingramcontent.com/pod-product-compliance
Lightning Source LLC
Chambersburg PA
CBHW051800230426
43670CB00012B/2366